THE DEFIANT IMAGINATION

WHY *Culture* MATTERS

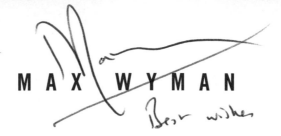

MAX WYMAN

Best wishes

The

DEFIANT

IMAGINATION

Douglas & McIntyre
VANCOUVER / TORONTO

Douglas & McIntyre Ltd.
2323 Quebec Street, Suite 201
Vancouver, British Columbia
Canada v5T 4s7
www.douglas-mcintyre.com

National Library of Canada Cataloguing in Publication Data

Wyman, Max, 1939–
  The defiant imagination : why culture matters / Max Wyman.

  ISBN 1-55365-007-7

  1. Arts and society—Canada. 2. Canada—Cultural policy. I. Title.
FC95.4.W95 2004   700'.971   C2003-907343-2

Editing by Barbara Pulling
Cover design by Jessica Sullivan
Text design by Val Speidel
Printed and bound in Canada by Friesens
Printed on acid-free paper ∞

We gratefully acknowledge the financial support of the Canada Council
for the Arts, the British Columbia Arts Council, and the Government of
Canada through the Book Publishing Industry Development Program
(BPIDP) for our publishing activities.

For the artistic community of Canada,
whose collective imagination over the past three decades
has enriched my life,
and the lives of many others, beyond measure

CONTENTS

PREFACE

*Life is all very nice, but it lacks form. It is
the purpose of art to give it some.*
— JEAN ANOUILH, *The Rehearsal*

THIS BOOK has gone through several incarnations on its way
into the hands of its readers. It began as a response to a challenge from a friend in government to articulate arguments
for public support for cultural activity; its original purpose was to
provide a platform for broad public debate of the issues involved.

It remains these things, but in the lengthy process of preparation
and rewriting it has become much more—a manifesto for wholesale
change in the way we as a society regard and value cultural activity.
After more than thirty years of writing and broadcasting about the
arts in Canada, I am more convinced than ever that we need a new
cultural contract between government and society, a contract that

places culture firmly in its crucial role as a catalyst for economic prosperity, social health and national identity, a contract that will help develop a nation of vision, innovation and generosity.

This belief has shaped and driven everything you are about to read. Parts of what I say may strike some readers as a statement of the obvious. Unfortunately, in an era of fiscal conservatism and lowest-common-denominator values, it still needs to be said. There has never been a more opportune or pressing time for Canadians to position culture at the centre of the social agenda.

In the jostling chaos of the modern Canadian metropolis—a chaos compounded by the pressure-cooker forces of immigration, urban development, housing crises, transit challenges, political volatility and the rapidly evolving virtual world—a new creative energy gives definition to cultural activity of all kinds.

However, none of this activity can properly be fostered until we see a wholesale shift in public awareness of its significance in a healthy democracy and a commitment on the part of Canadians to integrate that awareness into daily life. This book's central thrust is the belief that culture, like health and education, is an unassailable human right, essential to the social and moral well-being of the society of the future. While the book's structure allows for selective "dipping" according to the reader's particular interests, it also provides a sustained argument for action on the cultural front at a turning point in the evolution of Canadian society. It may enrage some and provoke others. Discussion is warmly anticipated.

M. W.

LIONS BAY, B.C.

JANUARY 2004

INTRODUCTION

The most beautiful experience we can have is the mysterious. It is
the fundamental emotion which stands at the cradle of true art
and true science.

—ALBERT EINSTEIN

W HY DO I CALL this book *The Defiant Imagination?* Because the imagination defies the constraints of expectation and the everyday. Because it is through the exercise of the imagination that we approach the realm of understanding that lies beyond the immediate and the real. Because it is in the act of imagining that we create what Yann Martel calls "an alignment of the universe along moral lines, not intellectual ones." Because the liberated imagination—liberated by engagement with cultural expression—is necessary to the achievement of all we hope for as a society.

Imagination puts us in touch with our moral sensibility, or what some call the soul: it leads us to the place where we can begin to establish what is right and what is best about the way we direct our lives. Terms like "soul" and "spirit" are heavy with troublesome freight, even looked on as suspect in rationalist quarters. But we should not shrink from using them, because they take us to the core of the discussion. Finding the right way forward is not simply a matter of rationality—doing the research, weighing the facts, making decisions. Facts can be misleading, as any afternoon spent in a criminal court can demonstrate. Imagination challenges the demands of the rational in its pursuit of moral truth. It lets us see that there can be better ways to live.

At its healthiest, society operates at a well-judged balance between the material and the non-material. We need food and clothing and consumer goods, all the trappings of the ordinary business of living in groups, in order to survive and thrive in a material way. But there are more things in heaven and earth than are dreamed of in a materialist's philosophy. The area of the intangible—the imagined, the intuited, the interior world of dreams—is where we discover who we are and what we might become. Our place in the continuum of being.

The imagination is the means by which we probe this mysterious and unknown realm. Reading, watching plays, looking at art—all the imaginative activities that occur when we share the cultural expression of others—is like plunging an arm into a vast, spinning barrel containing the untold millions of items that make up the accumulated wisdom of history. Who knows what scintilla of understanding we might catch and pull out of this whirling chaos, what knowledge we might find within our souls as well as within our minds?

To exercise our imaginations in this way is part of our search for significance within the greater cycle of being, our investigation of our relationship with the wondrous. It is, in the broadest sense, a spiritual search for ultimate meaning, one that might even be seen as a secular form of religious activity: an attempt, both alone and in the company of others, to make a connection with the transcendent, with something greater than ourselves.

We may never find solutions to these mysteries we probe, but in the act of venturing forth we become more developed, more questioning human beings. We educate ourselves about alternatives, and in the process consider other ways to arrive at the right way to live. It is a way, as Northrop Frye put it, to create the patterns that bridge the material and the spiritual world. A way of finding wisdom. Without the well-supplied imagination, without the inspiration that contact with creative activity can give us, we risk shortchanging ourselves in becoming the fully developed human spirit. We risk becoming less than it is possible for us to be.

LET US PAUSE a moment and take a breath. We are already at risk of casting ourselves adrift in a void of abstraction and ideal. How does all this translate into action and effect?

Even the most abstract piece of artistic expression can leave us with the feeling of having experienced something significant. Many of us have stood before a painting, listened to a piece of music or watched a piece of choreography and felt a sense of inexplicable, even inexpressible, understanding or revelation. Our emotions or thoughts— what we might even call responses of the spirit—may have no rational source, yet they reverberate within us with a strange conviction.

We feel odd at this moment, and—for a few seconds, before we put back on the shell we wear in our street lives—somehow enriched, privileged, warmer. These moments are spontaneous gifts that we could never replicate. The next time something similar happens we will be in another place: in a gallery standing before one of Jeff Wall's backlit, still-life photo-dramas, or in a movie house watching *Atanarjuat* (The Fast Runner), or in a quiet room reading *The Life of Pi*. We come to regard these moments as precious, secret prizes, yet they are available to us wherever art is made, so long as we are prepared to open ourselves to them. They are riches we can accumulate without number.

Seen like that, engagement with art is a way to furnish our minds. Perhaps we are not even conscious of the moment when it happens, but one day we find that a concept we never understood before has been planted in our thinking: we find ourselves measuring life in a different way. The story of Antony and his pursuit of Cleopatra might give new colours to our view of the lovesick. We see a production of *Hosanna* and empathize afresh with society's misfits. We look at the drypoint scratches of David Milne and are stirred by nostalgia for the hazy summer calm of the landscapes he evokes—even if these are landscapes we never knew.

Because it is not hemmed about by the corset of reason or logic, art can help us glimpse the truth of life beneath the veneer of civilization. It gives us a chance to examine our feelings or to express them in an intensified way. Books, plays, paintings, ballets, music ... all have the potential to express ideas and insights we have perhaps intuited but not been able to articulate. In its engagement with the emotional or moral perplexities of our age, a piece of art might call into question our most cherished beliefs, might prick our consciences or provoke our concern. Ultimately, we can look on our contacts with art as part of a personal search for authenticity, the hidden truths of our daily being. And the experience lets us know we are not alone in that search, even though the search may last a lifetime. The experience of art lets us see humanity in its ultimate defencelessness. It lets us know there are many ways to love and protect and celebrate what it is to be human: the holiness of the ordinary.

When looking at a painting we have to open ourselves to its influence and absorb it internally, not through intellectual dissection but through intuitive absorption. The real "message" of the work should be felt in the heart region.

—JOHN KOERNER, *Unseen Dimensions: Musings on Art and Life*

The experience of art diverts and entertains us, thrills and exalts us, provokes us to understand and to feel compassion. We value it, first and foremost, for its own sake; and its effect on the individual is an entirely personal thing. But stronger forces are at work here. Art can persuade us to alter our views, even challenge us to take specific action. And we would be naïve if we were to discount the social and political importance of artistic and cultural expression, particularly now.

Everything connects. Canadian culture, the imaginative expression of our shared lives and aspirations, is the heartbeat of our people. Its networks of influence are society's arteries. It is in the broad arena of our pluralistic culture that the stories that speak of Canada's distinctiveness are told. In the defiant imaginations of our artists we see the possibilities for our future; in the clamour of their voices we hear the sound of our unfolding identity. Our artists supply the raw materials of the imagination, the foundations on which wisdom and hope are built, for our young people and for Canadians everywhere. The stories we tell each other—in our plays, our books, our films—affirm the importance of the human, the local, the specific: they are the crackly bits that give society texture in the face of the blender forces of globalization.

The suggestions made in this book are founded in the positive belief that we can no longer afford to let the riches of this enormous natural resource go to waste. The human race is at a time of great moral and ethical challenge. We must deal with social and scientific advances fraught with promise and danger in equal measure. We are under intensifying pressure to come up with innovative responses to some of the most profound dilemmas humankind has faced. We are already managing global health threats badly, are often unable to protect human rights, have little control over the international flow of capital, and are nowhere near eliminating the curse of poverty or curing the world's environmental ills. Advances in scientific research—stem cell research, the human genome, cloning, robotics, nanotechnology, the promise of extended life, biotechnologies that empower individuals to slaughter entire civilian populations with the contents of a test tube—force us to re-examine our moral priorities as human beings. The new technologies risk creating new societies of haves and have-nots on the mere basis of access to the necessary machines. And everywhere we see the manifestations of exclusion: xenophobia, a distrust of "the other," an unwillingness to share, a closing of borders.

Questions about the role of creativity in a world that seems ruled by uncontrollable economic and political forces are not new. They have been debated since the end of the Second World War and the defeat of fascism. What has thrown them into such sharp relief today is the unprecedented potential of what our technological advances now make possible. As society comes to terms with these challenges and opportunities, decision-making will of necessity be based less and less on short-term political and economic opportunism and more and more on long-term moral and ethical choices. It is a process in which the informed and aware individual will play a crucial, perhaps unprecedented, role promoting social priorities. The values that will best guide us in the twenty-first century must in the first instance be humanistic rather than materialistic, concerned with dignity, freedom, true justice and the fully realized life. The social and economic structures of the new Canada will be built on innovative and imaginative solutions—humane, moral solutions—to problems we have not dreamed of yet.

Reason and science alone cannot guide us. Scientific truth cannot teach us about morality or ethical judgement.

Engagement with art synthesizes the rational and the emotional, the imaginative and the intuitive. It releases the visionary impulse, bringing an innovative dimension to problem-solving. It adds judgement and wisdom to information. Fie on the romantics who dismiss science as incidental to the grand moral plan; but fie, too, on the rationalists who discount the importance of humanistic inquiry.

As I examine in detail in a later chapter, engagement with artistic creativity develops the ability to think creatively in ways that significantly enlarge the educational experience. It encourages the flexible, nuanced thinking that will be an essential requirement of any innovative response to the challenges we face. It makes us see our world in fresh ways, encourages suppleness of mind. Doubt is cast on our most comfortable preconceptions. We learn the valuable art of adaptability.

The need to foster resources of imagination and intuition makes it vital that the culture and arts are central as we design the new relationship between technology and society. A diverse cultural expression that asserts the primacy of the human and the humane must be a fundamental component of the new Canada. And recognition of its relevance to all of us must be integrated into every level and department of our governments.

This relevance cannot always be quantified in ways that satisfy the number-crunchers. It is therefore sensible to exercise caution about the scope of what is claimed, and the chapters that follow should be viewed in that light. However, the growing demand from funders for hard data proving the social "goods" of cultural activity is forcing researchers and specialists to become increasingly engaged in a search for measurable evidence. Provision of that evidence will be a key element of any long-term campaign of advocacy and political persuasion on behalf of the arts and culture.

THIS ALL CARRIES great significance for Canada. As a community, Canada is an experiment in constant renewal, a welcoming society built in a spirit of democratic pluralism. We are finding that the experience and knowledge of a multicultural population with roots in many countries and societies is one of our great strengths. From that diversity flow insight, creativity, wisdom. Confidence in our culture and belief in its living, ceaselessly changing diversity gives us a communal ability to counter xenophobia and cultural paranoia.

Canada's cultural integrity will be a key issue confronting the nation in the coming decade. Faced with the threat of international cultural uniformity, we must affirm the diversity of our cultural expression, the uniqueness of the threads that make up our pluralistic nation. A strong, healthy cultural community, one that embraces all the possibilities the new knowledge economy can offer, is vital to the continued evolution of the Canadian identity.

The potential exists for Canada to reinforce, on the international stage, the value of a society built on compassion and shared values, in which widely different cultures can live alongside each other in a spirit of positive compromise and mutual understanding. Shared experiences, discoveries and values reinforce our sense of inclusion, foster mutual respect, and help different cultures understand one another. Here is where notions of generosity and respect can be laid out and questioned; here is where we can map the potential of what it means to be human in this fascinating and rapidly changing world.

None of this can be achieved without effort and investment. The Canadian cultural scene confronts great challenge and great opportunity in these early years of the new millennium. The challenge comes on many fronts: demographic (the changing face of Canada has already fundamentally affected our social and cultural fabric), creative (new forms of art-making are emerging, facilitated by the tools of the new knowledge society), technological (new delivery mechanisms hold much promise for our arts community), political (the process of globalization heightens the urgency of our need to assert our cultural distinctiveness), and structural (the cultural landscape has changed almost beyond recognition since our support models were designed and put in place, and it is beyond time for their overhaul).

How our artists and those who support them respond to these challenges will shape not only the cultural scene but all of Canadian society.

Although audience tastes and habits change from decade to decade, there is growing evidence that a renewed acceptance of the arts is emerging. In one sense, we are seeing a replay of the late 1960s and early 1970s, when an awakening Canada, sensitized by a variety of forces—the idea of identity that grew from the experience of Expo 67, the loosening of the colonial bonds that had held the country in thrall for so long, the emergence of Quebec from the grip of repressive politics and the Church, the steadily increasing threat of cultural colonization by a stronger neighbour—recognized that cultural expression was a vital aspect of who we are and what we can be.

This time, the stimulus is different. We live in a society of far wider technological potential, a society of greater cultural diversity, a society whose structures are in constant flux. But there are deeper reasons as well, reasons that are a complicated mix of apprehension, bewilderment and hope—the despair-inducing events of 9/11, the depersonalizing effects of globalization, the disconcerting yet exhilarating implications of the new technologies.

The effect of these pressures is to set us searching for new anchor points for our lives. The profit-driven modern marketplace is regarded by some with growing mistrust. Others find it unfulfilling. We search instead for connections with the human spirit. We can measure society's growing appetite for those connections in bookstores, in highschool courses and in online programs in creative writing. It is an appetite that must be nourished and encouraged.

Modern Western society assigns the arts a place on the fringes of our existence, yet the creative impulse is part of what makes us who we are as human beings. It is in our theatres, galleries, libraries and concert halls, at our community centres and our powwows, on our television and movie screens, in our schools and in our homes, that the limitless expression of the human imagination is displayed.

Access to this created living heritage of Canada is everyone's birthright. But for too long too many of us have neglected to exercise our claim to it. For decades the remoteness of the artist has been promoted almost as a virtue. It is vital now to reassert art's centrality in our shared lives, to eliminate that divide, to encourage every citizen to claim entitlement. The cultural community has a responsibility to renegotiate its significance to the society it serves.

Cultural activity belongs to everyone. It is simply an essential part of what it means to be human. Those who would hedge it about with exclusivity and excessive reverence, as if its blessings were a privilege only available to particularly insightful members of a private club, commit a kind of theft. We all have a share in art's riches, and we all have the ability within us to respond to its gifts.

Providing access to the arts involves more than driving a busload of kids to the theatre twice a year. Access is no longer a matter, as it was once described, of luring people into the sanctuary and whispering explanations in their ears as they stand there awestruck. Youth, minority cultures, the aboriginal community, people with disabilities, the people of the inner cities and the people of rural Canada: access is a right that belongs to us all, as ordinary—and as vital—as the right to read, the right to shelter. It is a matter of making available to all Canadians something that is integral to the fullest enjoyment of health, harmony and happiness.

Simply put, physical health is a necessity for life, but culture, the arts, our expressive heritage, are reasons for living, catalysts of our imaginations and prompters of our dreams. If we hope to make a full life, and to live that life in decency, freshness of curiosity and freedom of spirit, we must always remain open to the offerings of the defiant imagination.

If we can agree that these are worthwhile ambitions, we have found a useful place to start.

I

MAKING
the CASE

I

CULTURE, THE
HEARTBEAT OF A PEOPLE

What, we may ask ourselves, are we defending? We are defending civilization,
our share of it, our contribution to it. The things with which our inquiry
deals are the elements which give civilization its character and its meaning.
It would be paradoxical to defend something which we are unwilling to
strengthen and enrich, and which we even would allow to decline.
— Royal Commission on National Development in the Arts,
Letters and Sciences (Massey-Lévesque report), 1951

THE WORD "CULTURE" is booby-trapped with nasty surprises for the incautious, so let us state some parameters from the start, well aware as we do so that the flood of argument over the meaning of the term is hardly likely to be stemmed.

Culture is all the intangible elements of communal existence that, in sum, describe the diversity of a community and make it unique.

Culture is the collective awareness, experience and memory that we share with the people around us.

Culture is the set of values, assumptions and beliefs—intellectual, spiritual, emotional, moral, legal—that we agree to embrace as a community.

Culture is the way we as a society interpret and express those experiences, values and beliefs to ourselves and to the world.

Culture, like societies themselves, is a fluid, protean entity, forever in the process of evolution and discovery.

Culture, though it can be dangerously divisive, is the essence of the evolving civilization that we make together.

UNESCO's recent Universal Declaration on Cultural Diversity sums up those various elements of culture as "the set of distinctive spiritual, material, intellectual and emotional features of society or a social group, and all it encompasses, in addition to art and literature, lifestyles, ways of living together, value systems, traditions and beliefs."

Another popular definition narrows down the target somewhat: Culture is everything that is created of an artistic nature—the imaginative expression of civilization rendered visible, audible, tangible in plays and books and dances, films and recordings and sculptures, scores and scripts and videos ... the whole exhilarating panoply of the creative outpouring of human community.

Let us agree to deal here primarily with this narrower definition, always bearing in mind art's indissoluble relationship with the broader term. Artistic creativity, by this definition, becomes the tangible expression of the culture in which it exists, a living affirmation of the shared hopes and visions of a group of people who have chosen to live together. Artistic expression is all around us: in the streets, in the theatres, in the parks, in the bookstores. It is a birthright to which we all can lay legitimate claim.

At their simplest level, the arts—cultural activities—bring aesthetic pleasure and gaiety to our lives. We must never forget that essence of absolute joy, unjustified by any reason other than its existence. But the arts have other, less evident functions. By reflecting aspects of life and society, they help to explain who we are, to make our identity visible. They give us context, individually and collectively. They show us different points of view and different experiences. They lead us in new directions, let us try things on. They often ask questions we might not voluntarily engage with, uncomfortable questions we might not be able to handle in any other way. And while we can argue convincingly that culture is beyond politics, beyond economics, the nurturing and protection of any society's culture must be interwoven with a multilayered system of support that nourishes creation, encourages excellence (a definition we shall return to) and ensures the distribution of every conceivable form of art.

Art always reaches its peak where it becomes the life interest of a people.
—STEFAN ZWEIG

Cultural activity is integral to a sense of community, as a primal form of communication and a shared act of the imagination. It can be as private as a Haida song passed down through a family from generation to generation or as public as a Korean festival dance. It can involve curling up in a chair with the new novel by Ann-Marie Mac-Donald or being part of a community watercolourists' circle in Mont Tremblant. Shared experiences, discoveries and values reinforce the feeling of inclusion in society. The sense of self-worth and personal identity this sharing promotes leads us to identify with a community and with a nation; at the same time, it encourages mutual respect and helps diverse cultures understand one another. Sharing art makes a community more civilized.

There is also this: Whatever the theorists might wish or hope, the notion of a perfect society, one that subordinates the life of the individual to some abstracted social ideal, has no basis in reality. Nothing about our lives, save death, is immutable, and the future cannot be foretold. The ideal, whether Marxist or Utopian, fails to take into account the unpredictability of human existence. Variety of imaginative response is humanity's great glory, and it is the height of self-delusion to believe that the human spirit can be subordinated to a tidy social vision. Individual engagement with art proffers alternatives, presents old views from variant angles, provokes new ways of seeing and thinking and feeling. And in its celebration of the uniqueness of each individual, art stimulates the flourishing of a healthy, skeptical civil society.

We've Come a Long Way—or Have We?

HERE ARE EXTRACTS from the 1951 Massey-Lévesque report:

It is doubtful whether many Canadians could give the names of six Canadian composers, and the composers themselves, through lack of a Canadian periodical on music and of funds to establish an effective association, have little knowledge of what their fellow-composers in other parts of Canada are doing. There is no published history of Canadian music; there is no adequate library of music in Canada ... Only a small fraction of Canadian composition is available in published form and we are told that the larger and usually more significant works are unlikely ever to be published ...

This country is singularly deficient in concert halls, and in general the musical life of Canada is conducted in inappropriate and incongruous settings, in gymnasiums, churches, hotel rooms, school halls or in motion picture theatres rented for the occasion at ruinous cost ...

Facilities for advanced training in the arts of the theatre are non-existent in Canada. As a consequence, our talented young actors, producers and technicians must leave the country for advanced training, and only rarely return. Except in the few largest centres, the professional theatre is moribund in Canada, and amateur companies are precariously handicapped, through lack of suitable or of any playhouse.

And so the litany of neglect went on. By 1957, the year the federal government finally acted on the report's recommendations, matters were changing, to the point that Montreal critic Sydney Johnson, writing about a performance by the Montreal Theatre Ballet, felt moved to note he had been observing a "more mature outlook" and "a change in atmosphere" in the state of Canadian artistic expression. "This change has become apparent in the last 10 or 15 years ... It is a subtle change and although it has developed independently and at different rates of growth in each artistic field it is the same change wherever one looks—a reflection of the different mental outlook and the growing maturity of the average Canadian. We somehow seem to have made the discovery that the arts have come to stay as a permanent expression of our national life. This has astonished us almost as much as the realisation we are regarded elsewhere as an influential and independent world power."

Today, at the beginning of the twenty-first century, we are no longer so easily astonished. The arts have indeed become a permanent expression of Canadian life. Our cultural community offers a huge diversity of professional activity, much of it winning recognition at the international level. Experiment and innovation thrive alongside world-class presentations of the classics. Our writers, filmmakers, choreographers and visual artists bring Canada acclaim and renown, and Canadians have unprecedented access to the work of our artists.

However, more than fifty years on, it remains doubtful whether many Canadians could name six Canadian composers (of "serious" music, at least), and too many of our creators are still forced to work in incongruous or inappropriate venues. Not only does the high-art/low-art chasm still yawn; not only do our artists still struggle to make a living: we remain reluctant, despite all the evidence of its

primal importance both to individuals and to human society, to recognize culture as a central pillar of support in our lives together.

We continue to allow our educators to consider the arts an
expensive frill. We are suspicious of attempts to ensure that our
artists are able to create, rather than having to work in bars, wash cars
or—the lucky ones—teach. And we are only beginning to rise to the
challenge of making the work of our artists available to Canadians in
every part of the country. Much remains to be achieved.

> *La meilleure façon de faire mourir une ville, un village, une région, c'est*
> *de fermer ses écoles, ses bibliothèques, de sabrer dans les sommes déjà*
> *ténues allouées à la culture. La meilleure industrie de toute collectivité*
> *humaine, c'est encore sa culture, celle qui imprime son empreinte sur les*
> *valeurs de ses membres, sur leurs relations entre eux et avec l'extérieur, sur*
> *leur organisation de travail et leur capacité de produire ... La culture,*
> *c'est l'authenticité d'un peuple.* —NORMAND CAZELAIS, *Le Devoir*

Two (Other) Solitudes

IT IS A MATTER of historical misfortune that sometime in the last
century the popular concept of cultural activity was coarsened into a
combative, us-and-them matter of personal taste. Who was *us* and
who was *them* depended on which side you took on the high-art versus low-art battlefield. High art was Beethoven and Shakespeare and
The Ballet: it was lodged in the metaphorical ivory tower, and you
needed a shiny gold key to get in. Popular culture was anything that
ordinary folk liked: stuff that was easy to get (and easy to get at), stuff
you could enjoy without trying.

Today the communications revolution has made those boundaries
meaningless. Everything is available at the press of a mouse button. A
new global democracy of access has been created. Yet the ivory tower
still stands, daunting and unassailable to far too many.

Misunderstandings lie on both sides of the moat. Those who enjoy "popular" culture have sometimes been reluctant to think it worth developing a taste for "serious" culture, and they are quick to brand those who have as clubby exclusionists guarding access to something only the initiated can properly comprehend. The high-art audience, for its part, has sometimes been quick to disparage the easy accessibility of "popular" culture and reluctant to share art's more elevated treasures. (In Canada, this tone was unfortunately set by the Massey-Lévesque report: although the report was passionate and highly influential in its demands for the positioning of culture at the forefront of government responsibilities, it was a creature of its makers, and its definition of culture has, in retrospect, an uncomfortably elitist, Eurocentric ring.)

There is an element of we-know-better one-upmanship in both camps. The Roman poet Horace was proud to hate the common herd; the anti-elitist delights in disapproving of discrimination and calling those who dare to state preferences snobs. But it is far more complex than simply denying the right of others to their opinions and reducing the question to an either-or choice. Each approach cuts us off from the possibility of individual pleasure.

Still, opposition to government cultural spending comes in many forms. From time to time, for instance, the idea of some kind of voucher system is floated, usually based on the claim that public money spent on arts subsidy could be put to more effective use through the distribution of coupons that individuals would be able to spend on Canadian arts products of their own choosing. In a somewhat similar vein, two senior thinkers at the conservative economic think-tank the Fraser Institute recently voiced the idea that there should be a large reduction in government cultural spending and in the related public services, such as the CBC, the CRTC and the Canadian Television Fund. This, they argued, would release tax dollars to allow Canadians to choose the culture they wish to support, rather than have it chosen for them by politicians and bureaucrats.

The voucher idea founders on the hand-off factor. We elect our governments in order to be able to hand off the difficult choices and the tricky tasks, in the full knowledge that we as individuals are not likely to have either the necessary information or insights—or stomach—to be able to do them justice. This applies as much to cultural subsidy as to justice, national defence and sewers, and the fatal flaw in a voucher system for the arts lies in any assumption that it could do the job of fostering and making accessible the artistic life of our country, or any country. It would be the appearance of democracy without the benefit.

The user-pay argument is another common one, probably because it is so easy. Why (goes this argument) should the many pay for the pleasures of the few? But while it is easy enough to show that our arts organizations and cultural institutions don't have sufficient public support to pay for themselves, it is illogical to take the next step, as so many critics of cultural support do, and suggest that this lack of "market viability" means they should not be funded from the public purse.

Not everyone benefits from the public swimming pool, but we all pay for it. Very few individuals, in proportion to the size of our population, can take advantage of Canada's network of national parks, yet an overwhelming proportion of Canadians support their funding. Funding culture is neither an imposition of taste nor an act of charity—it is an investment in the health of the community, in the same way that building roads and hospitals is an investment in the health of the community. The value of amenities such as pools and parks (not to mention schools and libraries) is well understood, and no one complains about their inclusion in the tax base; yet, somehow, different standards apply when we assess the value of our creative community.

Culture and the arts are easy targets when it comes time to cut costs, and easy platforms for political grandstanding, as we have seen in recent years in the United States, where state and municipal funding has been consistently eroded. When elected representatives present the case as a choice between arts funding and improved hospital care, they are daring their constituencies to turn their backs on health in favour of the symphony—and at the same time demonstrating that they are serious about keeping budgets in check. It's an unpleasant business, they're saying, but someone has to do it, and don't you admire me for taking it on?

The professional arts community does not always help its cause. Assertions of entitlement and the tedious pleading of exceptional circumstances, generally at moments of extreme financial crisis, tend to alienate the common citizen. But the brute truth is that cultural activity, from the grassroots individual artist to the sophisticated machines of the national cultural industries, will never pay its own way, let alone turn a profit, not in many countries built on capitalist democracy, and particularly not in Canada, where we are acutely aware of the power of the cultural elephant across the invisible border. We have not always understood this. Initially, some saw funding initiatives such as the Canada Council for the Arts and the equivalent provincial bodies as relatively short-term activities that would build the kind of audience response and private sponsorship that would make public help unnecessary. But in the interim our society's evolution took a different turn. Mass media (largely foreign) found it could make huge profits from a small number of cleverly marketed artistic products (singers, movies, TV shows: largely foreign) while the rest of the creative community was left to beg for its supper.

Another reason for this disconnection between art and society lies in the idea that art doesn't need to have relevance. "Art for art's sake" is a fine-sounding slogan, and a useful one for those who want to assert the political inviolability of the creative act. But the meaning of the slogan has become distorted. It has become a defence of art without significance. If we wish to forge a new relationship between art and people—or to reforge the relationship that has always existed, however tenuous the connection has sometimes become—those on both sides of the moat must reassert art's centrality to our shared lives.

In the Shadow of the Elephant

MORE THAN FIFTY years ago, in its brief to the Massey-Lévesque commission, the Canadian Arts Council (precursor to the lobby group the Canadian Conference of the Arts, and not to be confused with the Crown agency, the Canada Council for the Arts) summed up the dilemma facing Canadians who wanted to make a life in art.

> Our small population, our wide geographical dispersement, and our bilingual culture make the commercial exploitation of any work of art—whether a book, a musical composition, a painting, a piece of sculpture, or a play—extremely difficult and, in most cases, unprofitable. This would be true even if Canada did not have the physical proximity to the populous United States, and the ties of language and tradition with France, the United States and Britain; but with the competition that springs from these sources it may safely be said that in no civilized country in the world do workers in the arts find conditions more difficult or rewards more inadequate.

Not much has changed. The need to assert our identity as a people has given Canadians concern for more than half a century. The encouragement of a Canadian culture that could resist what was effectively cultural colonization lay at the heart of the Massey-Lévesque report. It identified in particular Canada's vulnerability in cultural matters to the "impressive" influences of the United States. "There should be no thought of interfering with the liberty of all Canadians to enjoy them," it said. "It cannot be denied, however, that a vast and disproportionate amount of material coming from a single alien source may stifle rather than stimulate our own creative effort."

The report raised an early and important additional warning, one that paralleled the Roman satirist Juvenal's ironic comment two thousand years earlier that the masses are happy to ignore their civic responsibilities so long as they can have their bread and circuses. American mass culture was dangerous, the report implied, because it promoted the development of a passive, manipulable citizenry.

Prior to the publication of the Massey-Lévesque report, and the subsequent founding of the Canada Council for the Arts, the prime sources of funding for the arts in Canada were American: the Carnegie and Rockefeller foundations.

Fifty years on, the U.S. threat remains real, and if anything more acute. We live beside the most powerful grouping of cultural industries on the planet, all devoted to the widest possible dissemination of (and the largest possible profit from) American cultural expression. Canada, with its shared language and immediate accessibility, is a sitting-duck market for *Time* and *Salon,* Britney Spears and the New York Philharmonic, *Sixty Minutes* and Oprah, Richard Ford and Harrison Ford. U.S. mainstream culture is already part of our self-knowledge. It furnishes our dreams. And it becomes more and more difficult to distinguish the local from the imported. Jim Carrey, Mike Myers, Shania Twain and Céline Dion may be Canadian in origin. But to use their Canadian beginnings as a pre-emptive claim of owner-ship is to deceive ourselves. The phenomenon is somewhat less pronounced in Quebec, where language provides a barrier to the deepest influences of U.S. cultural colonialism, but in much of Canada, as polls have repeatedly shown, U.S. culture is often the culture we turn to first.

Canada is not alone in this dilemma. In Germany, the odds that a moviegoer will be able to see a German film are three in twenty; in France, the odds that a cinema will be screening a French movie are three in ten. But in Canada we have only a one in twenty chance to see a production that comes from anywhere other than Hollywood.

As for Canadian films, Statistics Canada figures show that, of the 110 million tickets Canadians bought for movies in 1998–99, less than 4 million were for Canadian features.

Some would argue that concern about U.S. domination of our markets and our means of entertainment is misplaced. And there is no doubt that globalization has a double edge. Its threat to the stability of nation-states (and to regions within or among them) is undeniable; neither the international flow of money nor global cultural colonialism take any account of borders. At the same time, curiously, increasing globalization seems to be provoking a fresh concern for the local. Canada's citizens shop the world and communicate globally via the Internet. They watch *Survivor,* drink Coke, wear Club Monaco. But they are also taking renewed interest in what is happening in their own backyards. From St. John's to Vancouver, Canadians are keen to affirm and protect whatever it is that makes their place their place. In an Environics poll in the fall of 2000, more than 80 per cent of people polled agreed that promoting Canada's artistic expression is essential if we are to remain a distinct country and that governments should ensure that artistic events are accessible to all Canadians. A Leger Marketing poll in the spring of 2002 showed that six in ten Canadians felt the prevalence of U.S. culture in Canada was a threat to our own culture's survival. As former Canada Council chair Mavor Moore once put it, "Canadians can't sing their own song if American commerce calls the tune."

Let us, in any case, not diminish what Canada is able to achieve in the shadow of the elephant. The success story of our publishers, assiduously cultivated by public funding for forty years, is by any measure astonishing. On a percentage basis, export sales of Canadian books exceed those of U.S. houses. Canadians bring home literary prizes almost as a matter of routine. The same happens in the cinema and the theatre. Robert Lepage entrances the world with his multimedia theatrics. François Girard captivates hearts and minds everywhere with *The Red Violin*. Zacharias Kunuk wins acclaim at Cannes.

Perhaps, in the end, this concern over the cultural independence of Canada will always be with us. More than seventy years ago, the Governor General, Lord Willingdon, privately expressed considerable misgivings about the "peaceful penetration" into Canada of U.S. media and economic influences. It *is* a peaceful penetration, and understandably so, given that the motivation is making a profit—indeed, the arguments advanced by the United States in support of open borders are all to do with the importance of freedom to trade. The trouble arises from the effect. The U.S. cultural steamroller, covering so vast a terrain, is a clumsy vehicle that can destroy or destabilize despite its drivers' best intentions.

The competition for screen time that Canadian creators must engage in with Hollywood is, in a practical sense, a competition for our sense of ourselves. For all the appeal of globalization's hybridity and cross-border reach, the individual continues to identify with a specific place—often the place of birth, but frequently an adopted home. The identity of that place is inextricably tied to the collective expression of the artists who live and work there. The images we look at, the music we listen to, the books we read—all contribute to our understanding not only of how the world looks but, equally, how the world operates and how it orders its values. The fewer of these images, sounds and books are Canadian, the smaller our chances of self-knowledge and self-assertion.

It would be foolish and misguided to try to close our doors to outside influence. Canadians would be much the poorer without exposure to the riches of foreign cultural expression. And what right does any government have to deny its citizens the right to choose what they consider to be the best that is offered, whatever its origin? But it is equally important, if we believe a cultural heritage helps to define a society's distinctive identity, that we do everything we can to develop local—that is to say, Canadian—cultural expression, at the highest possible level of excellence.

We must seek the point of balance (such a Canadian idea) at which we are open to those riches without letting our own diverse expression be swamped. To achieve that balance, we need to strengthen and protect Canadian art and Canadian artists. Internationally, you are what your culture shows you to be.

2

ART AND SOCIETY

*It is futile to argue about the importance of the arts in society on
grounds that accept the usual popular assumptions about that importance. The basis of all such assumptions is an unshakable conviction that
the arts are something we could do without: we may associate them with
something pleasant—beauty, special insight, world peace, or
whatever—but as soon as the social mood changes
such pleas are gone with the wind.*
—NORTHROP FRYE, *Art and Reality: A Casebook of Concern*

TWO OF THE MOST popular arguments advanced in favour of
society's support of cultural and artistic activities are these:
culture is an economic engine, and culture is an instrument
of identity and prestige. These are of course splendid arguments, full
of right-minded vigour and the hum of social progress.

The economic argument has proven particularly effective in convincing the bureaucrat, the accountant and the politician that the
return is worth the investment. And government increasingly per-
ceives that putting money into the arts and culture is not a matter of
frittering away hard-earned taxpayer dollars on the cultural equivalent
of a junk bond. Culture turns out to be a remarkably sound investment,

typically providing returns that would create paroxysms of envy in a mutual funds manager. Overall, the money invested by governments in the form of cultural subsidies is returned in multiples—cultural goods and services generate, in jobs, more than triple what is spent by the three levels of government on all forms of cultural support.

Specifics? According to the Department of Canadian Heritage, the arts and culture sector is the fastest-growing employer in the Canadian economy, worth $22.4 billion in jobs—a significant contributor to the nation's economic health by any measure. In the 1990s, jobs in Canada's cultural industries grew by 32 per cent, compared to a 12 per cent growth in the country's population. More than 700,000 people are directly employed in the arts and culture; that amounts to almost 5 per cent of all jobs in Canada, and employment for almost 3 per cent of Canada's population.

The impact is felt not only in the areas of performance and presentation but in service fields such as tourism: almost two in every five of the 7.5 million tourists who visited Canada from abroad in 1999 (and spent $15.3 billion in the process) took part in some form of cultural activity, according to national tourism indicators. And while a number of variables make it difficult to put a precise value on these benefits— What if the money were invested in other areas? How many full-time jobs are created? Would tourists still make their visits even if the cultural amenities were missing?—the overall effect is not in dispute.

The argument for culture as an instrument of identity and prestige has become a particularly popular one, for obvious reasons, in those areas of government dealing with international trade and commerce. "When the time comes for non-Canadians to buy, to negotiate, to travel, Canada's chance, or the attitude toward Canada, will already have been determined to a surprising extent by the projection of our culture abroad," wrote John Ralston Saul in a position paper for the federal government in 1995. Often, the decision to send Canadian artists abroad (the Royal Winnipeg Ballet on a tour of the Asia Pacific region, the Canadian Opera Company to the Edinburgh Festival, Janet Cardiff and George Bures Miller to the Venice Biennale) is influenced by their potential value as cultural ambassadors. In the words of Foreign Affairs Minister Bill Graham, Canada's artists project a vision of Canada as "dynamic, creative, open, multicultural, innovative, technologically advanced and tolerant … It gives us the opportunity to capture the imaginations of foreign opinion leaders, policy makers and business people with the quality of our creative work."

Though some might take issue with the commodification of culture that these arguments imply, they are prominent elements in the armoury of justification that politicians and bureaucrats employ when asked to address the vexed and vexing issue of cultural support. But these are by no means the only validations that might be offered on culture's behalf.

Those communities that are richest in their artistic tradition are also those that are the most progressive in their economic performance and most resilient and secure in their economic structure.
—JOHN KENNETH GALBRAITH

IN MY YEARS as a critic, I always hoped to come away from an encounter with a work of art in some way changed, with a different perspective on some aspect of how the world works. We yearn for ways to live better throughout our lives, as the brisk market in self-help books, videos and TV gurus attests; experiencing art is, in that sense, another means of checking out options for different ways to live. Entertainment, not instruction, may be what we initially seek when we watch Michel Tremblay's *Les Belles Soeurs* or read Carol Shields's *Larry's Party,* but we are often left with a proposition or two to think about. An afternoon spent contemplating the sinuous symbolism and delicate erotica of Gustav Klimt transports us to the boudoirs and backstage dressing rooms of nineteenth-century Vienna, lets us try on, for a while, the life and assumptions of a different time. Perhaps we let ourselves sink into the mystery and repose of Christopher House's *Persephone's Lunch,* a dance he created for Toronto Dance Theatre. It is inspired by Homer's *Odyssey,* but we are not anxious to make logical sense of its episodes of delirium and regret; rather, we let the elegantly extroverted physicality and decorous passion swirl together to evoke the human journey we all share.

Whatever it is we choose to engage with, we are embarking on an adventure into the unfamiliar. We might discover—too late—it is an adventure we would rather not have begun, and sometimes even an artwork that once entranced us can fail to speak to us on a second viewing. But it is a rare occasion when we cannot salvage something useful from the experience. The theatres, galleries, libraries and concert halls of the nation are the jousting grounds on which opposing views on a multitude of topics, and concepts of the Good and the Beautiful from many cultural sources, can show their mettle. Differing approaches to the world, differing ideas of morality and of the function of art, differing opinions on what constitutes professionalism in creativity, differing interpretations of excellence: through the expressive art of others we can test a hundred different notions that we would never have the chance—nor perhaps the effrontery—to test in our daily lives. Each time, through the act of seeing with the eyes of another, we amplify what we know of the life we live. We enrich the reality of our everyday.

So while the act of artistic creation is a singular human gesture that may be rooted in no more than the artist's drive for self-expression, it is impossible to separate that act from the effect it has on society, however remote the connection. The creative impulse is part of what makes us who we are. It adds to the sum of shared human experience, insight and knowledge. It also contributes, in a more general way, to social health—through the therapeutic values of art, through art's value as an educational tool and through art's ability to advance a more compassionate society.

The experience goes beyond the personal, yet it is in the personal that the process of change begins. And change is a process in which confrontation is bound to occur. In the long term, the experience has the potential to broaden and deepen the bounds of public taste and understanding. The discussion becomes more subtle as we examine why, as well as what. Acceptance of difference becomes easier. We recognize the validity of the other. Strand by strand, the fibre of our society strengthens. We see more clearly where we want to go.

Culture and Community: Bowling Together

AS CANADIANS, WE PLACE a high value on our public health care system, are proud of the way it makes Canada different and enviable as a society, and are willing to fight to defend it whenever it comes under threat. The value of cultural activity is less often discussed. Yet the strength and health of a community depend to a large degree on how committed individuals are to the well-being of their neighbours, and involvement with cultural activity fosters that sense of connectedness.

Modern communications methods make it possible to go for days without live interaction with another human being, and involvement with the arts, as either participant or observer, does much to counteract what Harvard University's Robert D. Putnam characterized as the "bowling alone" syndrome—a metaphor for the 1990s downturn in civic participation that sprang from the essential loneliness and disconnectedness of modern life.

The value of the arts in giving us a sense of shared interest and direction—and a better understanding of the other—has deep resonance for many Canadians. The previously quoted Environics survey showed that more than 90 per cent of Canadians felt the arts teach us about different cultures and ways of living, expose us to new ideas, and play an important role in helping maintain the country's cultural identity.

One of the most successful examples of a community-based arts endeavour is the city-reads-a-book movement that began in Seattle in 1996 and rapidly spread to Los Angeles, Chicago and then to Canada. Its essence is simple: library committees nominate a book that they ask every citizen to read.

In Chicago, the choice for the "One Book, One Chicago" campaign in the fall of 2001 was Harper Lee's *To Kill a Mockingbird* (ironically, a book that activists in Nova Scotia in 2002 tried to ban from schools for its allegedly racist use of language). Chicago's library officials envisioned "a nice little program [in which] we got strangers talking to strangers on trains and in coffee shops." Corporate sponsors were brought in. The city prepared a resource guide for teachers and distributed 40,000 lapel pins. The library held book discussions, and Starbucks provided free coffee and pastries for customers who participated. High schools performed theatrical versions of the story of a white lawyer who defends a black man accused of rape in a Southern town in the 1930s. The Chicago Bar Association held a mock trial of the courtroom drama depicted in the novel, in costume. The Chicago Public Library staged a screening of the movie version.

The result? The novel was checked out of public libraries more than 6,500 times in seven weeks, with librarians reporting that some patrons said they had not read a book for years, until the city's effort made them feel part of something bigger. The paperback made its way up from 250th to 51st place on amazon.com's sales list.

The program subsequently had a similar effect in Canada. The Vancouver Public Library chose Wayson Choy's *Jade Peony* for its first city-wide read, and brought the native son home from his adopted Toronto to participate. In the Kitchener-Waterloo region, the choice was *No Great Mischief,* by Alistair MacLeod. CBC Radio came up with a twist of its own, asking a group of celebrity experts to name a book they felt was worthy of discussion and eventually choosing Michael Ondaatje's *In the Skin of a Lion* as the book that Canadians would "read together" by means of national serial broadcast. The effect was immediate. Nationally, *In the Skin of a Lion* sold more copies in the two weeks following the announcement of its selection than it had sold in the previous year. It went to the top of the best-seller lists. And readers and book lovers realized afresh the values of a shared experience.

However, the idea of art in the community doesn't stop at shared book-readings. Where once we might have seen community involvement as a principal argument for community cultural activity, we see now that the arts can play a useful role in broader issues such as social justice, public safety and community revitalization—what is sometimes referred to as arts-based community development.

One of the best-known examples of the way the arts can reinforce a sense of community is the revitalization of the Granville Island area of Vancouver. Formerly an industrial wasteland beneath the two bridges that link the central city and its southern residential areas, Granville Island is now a hub of community activity. It houses, alongside the industrial activity that has always been its focus, several theatres, one of the country's most important art and design institutes, a thriving arts school for children and a wide range of artists' ateliers as well as a popular public market, a boutique hotel, restaurants and a community of floating homes and mixed-income housing.

Queen's Quay, in Toronto, with its theatres, fashionable shops and frequent festivals, is a similar example of creative revitalization through the arts. Another is the Newfoundland outport of Trinity, which for more than a decade has been home to the New Founde Lande Trinity Pageant, a festival staged by Rising Tide Theatre to celebrate the region's heritage. It is an event that both reinforces a sense of community and helps develop its economy. In Trois-Rivières, Quebec, a decision to use art and culture as a focus for community revival has led to the development of a thriving poetry festival, a program of architectural restoration and a strong emphasis on community involvement in music and the visual arts—all of it help-ing to reverse the decline of what was once a thriving industrial centre.

More than two hundred community volunteers have worked with three professional artists to create the largest public artwork in the history of Vancouver—Community Walls, Community Voices, *a 150-metre-long mosaic and concrete panel on a retaining wall stretching for three blocks along a busy city thoroughfare. Initiated by the Native Learning Centre, a college for the aboriginal peoples of the area, the project, under the leadership of artist Richard Tetrault, has blossomed into a multiracial collaborative venture that has allowed many individuals and groups to contribute to the overall theme of "origins." Twenty-eight mosaic medal-lions deal with everything from personal backgrounds to stories drawn from the history of nearby Trout Lake. "At first there was a certain degree of skepticism," Tetrault said. "Some people wanted to know who we thought we were to be coming into their neighbourhood. But what we hoped would happen, and what has happened, is all these different seg-ments of the community began to work together."*

Participation in artistic activity is quite different from being a member of an audience. Community artistic activity—a play, a col-lection of oral history, a show about local architecture—lets people see local problems from a different perspective. It not only teaches skills such as problem-solving, critical thinking and collaboration, it fosters reflection on ways to contribute to the greater good of the community. Through developing citizen involvement in local issues it encourages people to take action to help shape public debate and bring about change—emancipation through cultural engagement.

Vancouver choreographer Karen Jamieson has increasingly been incorporating groups of untrained individuals into her presentations, partly because she is interested in working with groups whose skills are at different levels, and partly because she thinks dance is "more than just a spectacle. It is also a way of thinking, and the more it permeates society, [the more] it will effect change, in a way that I think would be very positive."

Her Community Dancers group at Vancouver's Roundhouse Community Centre brings together individuals of varying shapes, ages and nationalities to work on dance ideas with Jamieson and other choreographers and to present performances. The people who attend have one thing in common: a desire to explore dance and feel the experience for themselves. Since Jamieson has spent many years investigating West Coast aboriginal mythology and performance, the group includes aboriginal artists, and its presentations, such as *Raven of the Railway,* staged in the summer of 2001, always have a strong aboriginal theme. In an interview in the Vancouver Dance Centre's magazine, *Dance Central,* in February 2002, Jamieson explained her continuing interest in aboriginal matters this way: "Part of what an artist is, I think, is a kind of cultural developer. We work in the field of culture, asking what it is and what it means. That is one reason why I am so interested in dialogue across cultures through my medium. You can then ask questions about the roots that connect us all."

A striking example of cross-cultural exchange through community involvement in art occurred during the creation of the Enderby Community Play in Enderby, B.C. The play, titled *Not the Way I Heard It,* chronicled the history of the community through an examination of the relations between aboriginal people and white settlers. A cast of 163 actors and musicians played 240 different roles, with another 500-plus helpers behind the scenes. Masks and puppets helped illustrate both aboriginal stories and tales of the settlers' struggles to establish themselves. "What strikes one most when sitting in the audience is the sense of companionship between the actors, musicians, crew and audience," said the local newspaper after the play's opening. "Not only does the play provide a night of laughter, but it also helps form a better understanding of who the citizens of Enderby are, and where they came from."

The project was part of a pilot art-in-the-community program on which a number of arts agencies collaborated. According to Cathy Stubbington, the project coordinator, the effect on the community was extraordinary. "The scale of the project was monumental, and the problems associated with bridging various ages, cultural, [and] economic gaps in the community brought [their] own series of conflicts and tension," she said. "But to see people come together during this process was incredible. People who would not have had much to do with each other before were suddenly working and playing together— and these relationships have lasted well beyond the end of the project. It's this kind of intangible effect that made it a magical process. People coming together to create art, especially for people who don't see themselves as artists, is an incredible tool. And now these folks have started thinking and feeling about art in new ways. Some of the youth involved have gone on to start their own theatre company and begun training in the arts. You can't begin to imagine the positive effect this process had on this community."

The success of projects like these highlights two issues critical to the success of community-based arts programs: the commitment of the participants and the clarity of the artistic vision. Equally important is a strong sense of community ownership of the project. It is not good enough, however well-intentioned the impulse, for an arts group to parachute in experts from outside equipped with someone else's vision of what is best for a particular locale. On-the-ground expertise and recognition of on-the-ground needs are essential.

In most cases this calls for prolonged and careful exploration by participating artists of each community's social structure and specific needs, and a willingness to work in partnership with community groups to make the project succeed. Understanding is also a two-way process: while art-based projects can be highly effective in addressing a variety of social issues in small communities, the communities themselves must be comfortable with the idea of working with artists. Time spent on building these relationships is a well-placed investment in building trust.

The Liveability Quotient: The Creative Class *and* la vie de bohème

WE CHOOSE TO LIVE in one place rather than another for a variety of reasons. Availability of congenial employment is an obvious priority; fortunate is the person who has no need to make that a consideration. But a mix of other factors also comes into play: geographic location (perhaps we want to feel near the centre of things, though the Internet is rapidly changing the need for that), the weather (some like it hot), the level of public services and public safety, environmental concerns, the availability of recreational spaces, the quality of cultural resources and cultural activity.

These are all factors that contribute to a city's "liveability quotient." And while it is true that cities thrive or decline in large part in relation to the diversity and buoyancy of their economies, cities that ignore the factors that contribute to this liveability quotient are at risk of losing the essential human capital that drives those economies. According to one study, the quality of life in a community increases the attractiveness of a job there by 33 per cent.

The availability and variety of cultural activity is a significant factor in the complex liveability equation. A growing number of studies show that when cities promote art, culture and heritage activities, they not only improve the quality of life for their citizens, but also attract the skilled workforce on which a vibrant economy depends. "Art and the city," says British historian Roy Porter, "achieve a magical synergism when [the city's] people look to artists to give them pride, identity, or at least a local language." Businesses increasingly locate in cities that both satisfy their needs for transportation, distribution and access to materials, and at the same time provide the cultural density and proximity to recreational facilities that will attract workers. Clearly, the cultural community has a pivotal role to play in helping to create this atmosphere of welcome and opportunity. Businesses also benefit from the presence of a healthy arts community in the sense that it provides a pool of on-the-spot expertise for support in areas such as design and marketing.

However, it is not only a matter of liveability. As we move towards a society in which imagination will supplant physical production as the basis of work, a city or region's economic health will increasingly depend on its ability to attract what has been called the creative class. In recent decades, an unprecedented culture of innovation has given rise to a class of creative professionals that includes scientists and engineers, poets and architects, doctors, software designers, writers and choreographers. In the U.S., this class is estimated to comprise 30 per cent of the workforce, and there is no reason to suppose that proportion would be any smaller in Canada.

Although these individuals do not necessarily regard themselves as a class, what they have in common is the ability to add creative value to society, contributing to a climate of innovation and economic growth. They also demand, as a group, certain characteristics in the places they choose to call home: not just the traditional elements of "liveability," but an openness to eccentricity or difference, cultural diversity, and an active, participatory, multidimensional lifestyle with a youthful orientation.

These elements of openness, acceptance and diversity are of particular interest here. To attract members of the creative class, cities are beginning to invest less in traditional infrastructure—retail malls, sports complexes and industrial zones—and more in people-oriented amenities: parks, performance spaces and galleries. Equally, cities are coming to understand that embracing diversity is key in attracting the creative class. "Many highly creative people, regardless of ethnic background or sexual orientation, grew up feeling like outsiders, different in some way from most of their schoolmates," says Carnegie Mellon University's Richard Florida, who has done extensive work in the area of quality of place and the new economy. "When they are sizing up a new company and community, acceptance of diversity and of gays in particular is a sign that reads 'non-standard people welcome here.' "

Florida's theories about this specific social group and its importance to a city's well-being have become well known in recent years; his pronouncements have taken on something of the quality of Holy Writ in some parts of North America's social planning community. But it is worth recapping them briefly here because they provide a useful launch pad for a discussion of art and culture in the city—even though it is clear that he has in mind far more than artists per se in his definition of the creative community.

In his book *The Rise of the Creative Class,* Florida tries to turn what *The Economist* has called "the geography of cool" into hard-numbers reality. He cites a number of studies that seem to demonstrate that there is not only (as has long been known) a connection between creativity, "bohemian diversity" and a vibrant city life, but that the presence of a concentrated grouping of "bohemians" creates an environment that attracts other talented or creative individuals.

Creativity equals capital. —Artist and political activist JOSEPH BEUYS

His use of the term "bohemian" is specific. It embraces individuals and social groups who might formerly have been marginalized because of their lifestyles and work ethic—writers, designers, musicians and composers, actors and directors, crafts folk, painters, sculptors, printmakers, dancers, and so on. Now, Florida argues, these people are becoming integrated into the mainstream of society and the economy, to the point where they provide a core around which other creative activity (particularly in the high-tech industry) clusters.

In the U.S., he points out, ten of the fifteen metropolitan areas with the highest concentration of "bohemians" number among the country's top fifteen high-tech regions. Cities with high immigrant populations and large gay populations show a similar relationship with the high-tech industry. When Florida and a Canadian collaborator applied his theories to Canada, the same statistical linkages held true. Not surprisingly, the Canadian cities that scored highest were Toronto, Montreal and Vancouver. All three are well known to feature the elements that, according to Florida, generate prosperity in the new economy: technology, talent and tolerance (for immigrants, gays and "bohemians").

In other words, the greater the diversity and visibility of cultural involvement, the more a community is likely to thrive. In the U.S., where more studies have been done on these matters, it seems also that urban revitalization projects work best in communities with a strong arts and culture presence.

Florida's definition of the "creative class" goes far beyond the cultural community, and it is difficult to give specific measurement to the social impact of the arts. Nevertheless, it seems logical that every level of government enrich the urban cultural fabric. Innovative, accessible and broad-based arts activities clearly constitute an integral element of any serious approach to the revitalization of our cities. The creative element is key. It embraces equally the work of scientists and artists, the solvers of problems and the askers of questions, and that cross-fertilization should be encouraged.

So far so good. In Canada we have already seen the development of strong arts and culture programs in many cities and municipalities. In 2002 the federal government recognized those advances by launching its Cultural Capitals of Canada program, which annually singles out and celebrates cities for their commitment to arts and cultural activities and holds them up as examples for other communities to emulate.

This is a useful step towards improved advocacy. Particularly valuable, beyond the cash award and title, is the encouragement the award gives to collaboration between a city's government, the private sector and the arts and cultural community to improve the climate for the arts.

But Florida's studies clearly imply that if we want safe, attractive, economically thriving communities in the coming century, we should give serious attention not only to investment in all forms of creativity but to the nurturing of a society of acceptance and openness. If we wish to develop cities that attract the creative class, understanding and open-mindedness play as important a part as the building of super stadiums and even opera houses.

People who take part in cultural activities are more involved with the life that goes on around them. They are more likely to identify with their community and develop a sense of pride not only in the place itself but in their place within it. The people of East Vancouver, for example, have an intense sense of ownership in connection with Illuminares, an annual summertime parade around a lake in a community park. Hundreds of individuals from many different city neighbourhoods gather for a procession featuring homemade lanterns in fantastical shapes, stiltwalkers, fire sculptures, torch choreography and fireworks. The event has been organized since 1985 by an organization fittingly known as Public Dreams.

The Dragon Boat Festival that takes place each year on Vancouver's False Creek serves as another powerful unifying force among the city's many cultures. Activities of this kind encourage the creation of intercommunity groups and friendships, built around shared interests and common concerns, and help individuals to explore creativity and enhance their self-esteem. They have the potential to lead a community to fresh possibilities and fresh strategies for their achievement.

All of this is highly attractive to the modern city, which is challenged by the technological revolution to make itself as inviting as it can to the skilled, plugged-in workforce that will drive the information economy of the coming century. Location still counts, but not for the same reasons. The liveability factors identified by Richard Florida are among today's key urban assets.

Canada is well placed to benefit from these social opportunities. Canadian cities that have actively worked to integrate the cultural expression of immigrant and aboriginal peoples into their social affairs programs, through festivals and art exhibitions, already note a marked improvement in cultural respect and understanding. As Vancouver mayor Larry Campbell puts it: "Our cultural diversity brings exceptional variety and vibrancy to our arts and culture sector, and stimulates ideas and dialogue in every area of civic life. Diversity fuels our world view, and gives us a distinct perspective on global as well as local issues and events." Florida holds up Toronto as an ideal example of the kind of urban balance he advocates, a city where the "boho factor" is high and where immigrants, artists, and gays and lesbians can fit in and feel safe without abandoning their cultural heritage or lifestyles.

The argument here is clear: Cities that thrive in the twenty-first century will be cities that pay attention to developing a true diversity of human creativity. That means not only more (and more accessible) public art, but a new attention to creative alternatives in development—ageing buildings rehabilitated into artists' studios and living spaces, for instance, rather than demolished to make room for a new batch of condos; the creation of multi-purpose cultural meeting places/showcases in the heart of downtown.

In many cities across Canada, visionary planners are already moving towards a new focus on the creative class and the cultural milieu. But they cannot do it alone. What is also needed is a new culture of collaboration between business and the creative community. Developers, chambers of commerce and boards of trade have powerful voices; their enthusiasms must be mobilized to help weave the many colours and textures of culture deep into the fabric of the city.

Culture and Social Change

ALL ARTISTS ARE SHAPED by their times and their individual circumstances. But the reverse can also be true. Because artists tend to use unorthodox, often intuitive means to question the status quo, their work can alert society to new ways of thinking about how we organize, govern and explore our lives together.

In his book *Cities in Civilization,* Peter Hall sets out to identify the factors that helped create the "golden ages" of creativity in six European cities, each of which he believes could fairly claim to be the great creative city of its time: Athens in the fifth century BC, Florence in the fifteenth century, London at the end of the sixteenth century, Paris and Vienna at the turn of the nineteenth century, and Berlin in the 1920s.

While Hall is careful not to paint with too broad a brush, and while we should not oversimplify his cautious discovery of the salient elements, certain factors tend to recur in his stories of the creative flowering of these cities. These include the following: A level of affluence that allows the community to "afford the luxury of art." An amenability to art and thought that accumulates over generations in a people living together. A high level of civic pride. A susceptibility on the part of that society to economic or social transformation, and a consequent atmosphere of uncertainty that encourages creative speculation. An element of serendipity, in terms of encounters and influences, that is nourished by the proximity of city living. And the existence of a class of "outsiders," creative talents drawn to the city by the foregoing factors but at the same time rebelling against its limitations.

It is interesting to apply these criteria (which do not necessarily all occur in each of the cities he mentions) to the development of the arts in Canada. No Canadian city has yet produced an equivalent "golden age" of creativity, of course, but where this exercise immediately leads us is to Montreal. Specifically, Montreal in the three decades following the Quiet Revolution of the 1960s.

This was, first and foremost, a society undergoing radical political and religious transformation, with all the concomitant social tensions that such changes bring. When Jean Lesage and his entourage swept to power on a tide of economic and cultural enfranchisement in 1960, proclaiming "It's time for change" and affirming that the Québécois were now "maîtres chez nous," they were asserting the primacy of a populace that had been kept for generations under the dominance of a repressive state and a conservative religious power. For the first time in modern history, the people of the province had the freedom to question received views, express themselves openly on political issues, and even test the strength of their ties to the Church.

What had also been maturing in the deep background was an artistic community—a community of "outsiders"—ready to give voice to this restlessness. Stirrings of resentment had been signalled as early as the 1940s. In 1948, the group of revolutionary young Quebec artists known as *les automatistes,* with Paul-Emile Borduas at its head and André Breton's *Surrealist Manifesto* as its brandished text, gave voice to that resentment in *Refus global,* a strident, passionate demand for a new social order. The same year, playwright Gratien Gélinas confronted (though more subtly) the same topics in his play *Tit-Coq,* about an illegitimate young soldier's search for acceptance in polite society. (Also in 1948, Saskatchewan, half a country away, created Canada's first provincial arts council and North America's first arm's-length arts funding agency. Two solitudes indeed.)

Part of *Tit-Coq*'s success lay in its use of the Québécois working-class vernacular, *joual*; it let the ordinary people of the province know that their concerns and this language were important enough to command the stage. Part of the shock of *Refus global* lay in its denunciation of the restraints imposed on the hermetic Quebec society by reactionary politicians and clerics. For their day, these were significant and daring messages, though it was not until Lesage's coup of 1960 that they were widely heard.

By that time, the creative class of Quebec, stirred by the intellectual input of immigrants from post-war Europe, was in a state of simmering, barely restrained tension. When the moment of release came, Quebec society and its artistic "outsiders" entered into a remarkable tacit pact: the artists would help consolidate the popular will, asserting the new-found identity of the Québécois; and society would permit, even encourage, its artists to explore new and formerly taboo realms of creative expression. The reverberations shook Quebec society to its foundations; they are still being felt.

Poet-songwriters such as Félix Leclerc, Gilles Vigneault and Robert Charlebois, and playwrights such as Michel Tremblay (who followed Gélinas's lead and put *joual* on the stage), became the public voice of a generation impatient for social affirmation and liberation. The province's young choreographers plunged headlong into topics, such as sex, politics and the Church, that had formerly been off limits. A new awareness emerged of the way the arts could influence the thinking and attitudes of a people. Claude Jutra, Marie-Claire Blais, Jean-Paul Riopelle ... artists became heralds and heroes of social change: they were giving visible, audible form to the new society.

The serendipity factor was undeniable. In the tight-knit artistic community of Montreal, it was impossible not to know and be influenced by what your colleagues were doing. The sense of being a creative "outsider" with a licence to rebel was also a liberating, even intoxicating influence. And Québécois society itself was more ready to listen to these cries for a new order than it had ever been. At the same time, the ideas and creative influences of Europe, particularly Paris, imported by immigrants and brought home by travelling Québécois, had persuasive play. For all these reasons, the Montreal artistic community became the most dynamic and most distinctly defined in Canada. It had character because it had cause, in a way that has been matched by no other Canadian city's artistic community.

This might not amount to a "golden age" in global terms. Much of the creative product was raw and unschooled. In modern dance, for instance, the new generation of choreographers, with little in the way of established teaching tradition to build on, were forced to make it up for themselves as they went along. But even this was a fortuitous circumstance, since what resulted was a visceral, high-energy movement style that gave visible form to the dynamic excitement of the new social order.

Art and community conspired to create both a new society and the *image* of that new society: audacious, multifaceted, increasingly pluralistic, filled with pride and hope. And that symbiotic relationship between art and community is reflected still in the province's generous support of the arts and culture: a recognition of the importance of creativity in the affirmation of a distinct identity.

Because of Montreal's unique position as the principal community inside a province that is considered by many of its residents to be a self-contained society, the city has developed a cultural distinctiveness unique in Canada. This is at least in part due to the enlightened vision the provincial and municipal governments share of the role cultural expression plays in the development of civic character—and not only within the cultural community, where one would expect it to be a veritable mantra. When the Montreal Metropolitan Chamber of Commerce held a symposium to consider the shape of Montreal fifteen years hence, the importance of culture in the city's growth was widely emphasized. When you speak of economic development, said chamber president Guy Fréchette, you have to recognize that culture has as much of an economic impact as big business. Quebec, which consistently tops the provincial tables in terms of per capita funding for the arts, also leads the way in terms of municipal enlightenment. Across the province, 43 municipalities and 23 regional districts have articulated cultural policies; Drummondville, for instance, with 47,000 inhabitants, devotes 5 per cent of its total budget to culture.

The province's cultural leaders are committed to the democratization of culture, on the grounds, as Culture Minister Line Beauchamp explains, that "a city in which the arts and letters don't have the 'freedom of the city' is deprived of its soul, of that vision that lets its people be stirred in unison."

There is no reason why other cities in Canada cannot benefit in a similar way from the contributions of their cultural communities. But it will not happen until our civic leaders make culture a central plank in their campaign for social improvement. This returns us to the notion of culture as a basic human right, culture as an essential element of our everyday, culture as a necessary pillar of our society's well-being and our lives together.

Bridging the Ingenuity Gap

THE ABILITY TO THINK creatively is a fundamental requirement in the knowledge economy of the new century, for the well-being both of society itself and of the individual wishing to participate productively. But social well-being is threatened by what the Canadian writer Thomas Homer-Dixon has termed the "ingenuity gap"—that is, the chasm between the need for innovative thought and our ability as a society to provide it.

Homer-Dixon, whose book on the topic won the Governor General's Literary Award for non-fiction in 2001, suggests ingenuity gaps widen the gulfs of wealth and opportunity within and between societies. He believes global stability will be threatened by the growing disparities between those who adapt well and those who do not.

The danger, he argues, is that our technological, social and ecological advances will outstrip our understanding of how best to harness their potential in the service of global affluence and equity. In our eagerness to embrace all that the new technology can give us, we may find ourselves bulldozed into violence by crises brought on by those very advances—crises to do with population growth, the way we treat the natural world, the way we distribute wealth and dispense justice. As the problems multiply, we find ourselves under intensifying pressure to come up with innovative ideas and solutions.

"We need imagination, metaphor and empathy more than ever," Homer-Dixon concludes, "to help us remember each other's essential humanity." He calls this "the central challenge of the coming century—one that will shape everything else about who we are and what we become." We cannot deal with this challenge solely by the exercise of reason. We must instead use our unique capacity to integrate emotion and reason, "to mobilize our moral sensibilities, create within ourselves a sense of the ineffable, and achieve a measured awareness of our place in the universe."

Those goals might as fittingly be used to characterize the making and experiencing of art. And that is as it should be, since it has been repeatedly proven that lifelong involvement with the arts is one of the most effective ways to encourage original thinking.

I would teach children music, physics, and philosophy, but most importantly music, for in the patterns of music and all the arts are the keys to learning.
—PLATO

Studies from Harvard and elsewhere show that hands-on experience of the arts in the school years is invaluable in developing individual creativity, self-expression and all manner of skills that are important to the way we work and live together in the twenty-first century. As Howard Gardner argues, we have multiple intelligences—mathematical, linguistic, spatial, kinesthetic, interpersonal, intrapersonal—and children learn in a multitude of ways. We know that a student's involvement with group performance—a play, an orchestra—leads to better motivation, an improved concept of the self, greater acceptance of others, better notions of team spirit and an improved understanding of broad social values. We know that problem students often excel at arts learning and go on to succeed in other areas. We know that the whole-person involvement demanded by artistic creativity has a deeper educational value than simply knowing the answer. "Children are powerfully affected by storytelling, music, dance, and the visual arts," says U.S. researcher Karen A. Hamblen. "They often construct their understanding of the world around musical games, imaginative dramas, and drawing."

Many studies have shown how exposure to the arts enhances student performance in other areas of education. A recent report from the U.S. Arts Education Partnership, a coalition of more than one hundred national educational, arts, philanthropic and government organizations, offers evidence that schoolchildren exposed to drama, music and dance may do a better job of mastering reading, writing and math than those who focus solely on academic subjects. The report, based on an analysis by James Catterall, education professor at the University of California, Los Angeles, of 62 studies of various categories of art by nearly 100 researchers, suggested that arts education could be particularly helpful to poor students and those in need of remedial instruction. "While education in the arts is no magic bullet for what ails many schools, the arts warrant a place in the curriculum because of their intimate ties to most everything we want for our children and schools," he said.

The Arts Education Partnership assigns the following benefits to the inclusion of specific art forms in the school curriculum:

- *Drama.* Helps with understanding social relationships, complex issues and emotions; improves concentrated thought and story comprehension.
- *Music.* Improves math achievement and proficiency, reading and

cognitive development; boosts verbal skills for second-language learners.

- *Dance.* Helps with creative thinking, originality, elaboration and flexibility; improves expressive skills, social tolerance, self-confidence and persistence.
- *Visual arts.* Improve content and organization of writing; promote sophisticated reading skills, interpretation of text, reasoning about scientific images.
- *Multi-arts* (combined art forms). Helps reading, verbal and math skills; improves the ability to collaborate and higher-order thinking skills.

A U.S. study of medical school applicants showed that 66 per cent of music majors who applied were admitted, compared to 44 per cent of biochemistry majors.

Engagement with art helps students to conceptualize, solve problems, communicate, reason, work effectively with others, allocate resources, integrate seemingly unrelated elements into a cohesive whole, make spontaneous decisions, use intuition. It improves confidence, creativity, discernment, originality, and resistance to closure (keeping ideas alive and creating supple minds). It develops a willingness to see problems from different perspectives. The learning is in the doing. Art instruction in schools has been shown to help develop reading, literacy and writing abilities, skill in mathematics (although recently somewhat discredited, the celebrated "Mozart effect" study, for example, showed that students who first listened to a Mozart sonata scored higher on tests in spatial-temporal skill, an essential element of reasoning in mathematics, physics and engineering, than students who did not) and other cognitive skills, as well as develop a deeper motivation to learn and improved social behaviour. As James Boyle, chairman of the Scottish Arts Council, put it recently:

Whether a child wants to become an engineer or a singer, the process of creative expression and performance is essential to complete development of the mind ... The arts experience ought to be in a continuum of learning, practising and performing (or exhibiting). Indicating horizons to be reached is a big part of education; the long perspective might be career, the medium term might be exams but the most tantalizing horizon is the one set by the self in creative activity ... Presentation of the self is the fundamental action in society. It may be manifest in the manner or the skills of a job interview but it begins in self-confidence, the sort of thing learned from the arts in performance and creativity.

Working in the arts in the classroom, the student learns and tests future workplace behaviour. Self-validation, improved confidence, openness to new ideas, a continuing curiosity about life—these are all by-products of exposure to art-making that CEOs of major corporations tell the directors of our art schools they value. Business leaders, like the more enlightened politicians, recognize that it is no longer enough to apply rational analysis to the challenges of the modern age. They need to develop a vision of what might be: to intuit solutions, rather than merely deduce them. This is where art and culture can help. It is a realm of activity that exists between the economic and the social, between the real and the imagined. Or, to put it more practically, the exercise of the imagination turns knowledge into wisdom, and wisdom into insight, and insight into progress. So they look, these CEOs say, for graduates with a sense of creativity, graduates who can analyze and synthesize, who see the connectedness of human society. In a word, innovators.

Business leaders also know that the old top-down command structure does not work in today's intensely competitive markets. Leadership is as much about working with others as it is about taking control. Collaboration and networking are increasingly significant elements of corporate success; so are unbridled curiosity and a willingness to share innovative ideas and lead through communication. Innovation is as much a social process as an individual one, and a corporation's location close to others working in the same field facilitates the sharing of experience and imagination.

Canada's youth are already at the forefront of the massive global communications change, comfortable with the new networking technologies and adept in their use. Enabling that new generation to make maximum use of the creative stimuli the arts provide is everyone's responsibility.

> *Of course we want kids who can read and write and do math. We also want them to be literate, culturally enlightened and environmentally aware … We need … to define a new set of basic skills suited for the information age and re-engineer our public schools to produce them.*
>
> —GUY SAINT-PIERRE, former Quebec education minister
> and chair of the SNC-Lavalin Group, in a speech to
> the Collegium of Work and Learning in May 2000

> *A nation without a vibrant creative labour force of artists, writers, designers, scriptwriters, playwrights, painters, musicians, film producers, directors, actors, dancers, choreographers, not to mention engineers, scientists, researchers and intellectuals, does not possess the knowledge base to succeed in the Information Economy, and must depend on ideas produced elsewhere.*
>
> —SHALINI VENTURELLI, specialist in international
> communication policy, American University

Arts Education: Planting the Seed

ENCOURAGING INVOLVEMENT with the arts at a young age has the potential to create a more receptive adult audience, which is certainly a tempting argument for any organization facing a threat of dwindling audiences. Marketers for the arts are discovering that crucial factors affecting cultural preferences in adult audiences are rooted in childhood experience—values transmitted by the family, values transmitted at school, childhood exposure to the arts and practising an art form as an amateur (though Lynda Hill, artistic director of Theatre Direct, which specializes in theatre for teenagers, speaks for many when she warns: "It's not about viewing the child as a marketing possibility or as part of the next generation of theatregoers. It's about making work that will speak directly to that child").

Another linked and equally tempting argument is that arts education creates a climate of endorsement. An individual who has learned to appreciate the arts from an early age is likely to have a more sympathetic view of their support as an adult. Arts education contributes to the accumulation of public will.

Other arguments have to do with employability and cultural pluralism. For all the reasons we have just examined, arts education helps develop individuals who bring valuable life skills and work skills to their employment. It also helps develop an awareness of other cultures and thus builds a more open and accepting society.

These are valuable considerations. Most significant of all, however, is the way interaction with the arts enriches the human individual, a process that starts at the earliest age. Social and cultural topics come into play; so does the development of critical thinking. Creative activity and a familiarity with the cultural heritage of humanity develop a sense of wonder, curiosity and reflection that opens the young mind and spirit, seeding the development of involved and creative citizens.

In 1998, the governor of Georgia, Zell Miller, inaugurated a fund to provide a recording of classical music to the parents of all 110,000 babies born in the state each year. The recording's title: Build Your Baby's Brain Power through the Power of Music.

For too many decades we have let our responsibilities to our young people languish. Despite the often heroic efforts of individual educators who find ways to communicate the values of culture and the arts to their charges, it is impossible today to say with any conviction that our school systems treat education in the arts and humanities with vision and insight. Generation after generation of students graduate from our schools with only the faintest notion of the riches that are rightfully theirs. Most provinces and territories have articulated impressive statements of principle regarding the inclusion of the arts in the school curriculum. But as economic pressures have intensified, the teaching of arts and culture to the young has increasingly been seen as a non-essential element of the curriculum—a subject that can be shoehorned into the class timetable as an option after the so-called basics are properly taken care of. Because of that it has become regarded as the refuge of the mediocre and incompetent, or as something anyone can do, and it should be a matter of shame to the entire country that no systematized approach, built on deep-rooted recognition of the long-term values of a broad grounding in cultural studies and the liberal arts, yet exists in our education system.

The difficulties in winning recognition for the importance of the arts and humanities within the school curriculum have been intensified at the national level by the issue of the "ownership" of education, for each of Canada's provinces and territories is at liberty to establish its own norms and practices. However, the situation is not entirely beyond hope. Many possibilities exist for culture and education to advance on a shared front. Repeated attempts to slip free of these political handcuffs have been made, and a concerted effort is currently underway to evolve some form of pan-Canadian standards, along the lines of those already developed in the math and science curricula by the Council of Ministers of Education, Canada (CMEC).

The National Symposium on Art Education (NSAE) has since 1997 brought together educators, artists and arts administrators to work towards some form of consensus on arts education principles and practices. It produced two pioneering documents articulating both a vision for arts education in Canadian schools and a framework on which that vision could be brought to reality, and urging CMEC to ensure that the arts are "a fundamental and sustained part of the Canadian school system for all students and in all schools." Late in 2003 a Coalition for Arts Education in Canada (CAEC) was developed out of the work of NSAE, with the intent to provide a national voice for arts-education initiatives.

The goodwill necessary to endorse these changes exists. Ninety per cent or more of the fifteen to twenty-four age group in a recent Canadian survey agreed that government has a responsibility to make artistic activities accessible to all Canadians. They felt that learning about music, drawing, acting and other art forms is important for children; believed that promoting and supporting Canada's artistic expression is essential if we are to remain distinct as a country; felt that artists and works of art play important roles in helping maintain the country's cultural identity; and agreed that the arts teach us about different cultures and ways of living.

Even if CMEC and CAEC are able to foster pan-Canadian thinking about an arts curriculum, however, substantial questions remain unanswered. Would there be testing? One school of thought suggests that cultural activity should be nurtured, not tested or graded, if we wish to develop a truly empathetic humanity in a multicultural world. But even if testing were to be instituted, what would be tested, and how? CMEC has begun to address the question of testing in core subjects, specifically including reading, math and science, in its Pan-Canadian Assessment Program, and that program is designed, says CMEC, so that other subjects, including the arts, can be added "as the need arises." But if a national curriculum with national standards were to be designed, what would that mean to specific local needs?

In the face of this continuing uncertainty, a number of significant arts-education initiatives have evolved outside the formal education system, though often working in collaboration with educational partners. In the past decade, for instance, youth involvement has become a core concern of the Canada Council for the Arts. In close collaboration not only with its professional arts partners but with other branches of government, the Canada Council encourages arts groups to invest in their own future through outreach programs that involve the placement of professional artists as trainers in the community. (The Canada Council's role in arts education is discussed more fully in a later chapter.) And most provincial education ministries actively encourage their schools to participate in the artist-in-the-schools programs that have proliferated in Canada.

One of the most imaginative and successful of these programs—certainly the most extensive in Canada—is Learning Through the Arts (LTTA), organized by the Royal Conservatory of Music. Launched in 1995 in nine Toronto schools, by the fall of 2002 it was involving almost 300 artists in a program serving close to 50,000 students in 185 schools in Canada and abroad (including three schools in East Harlem and 24 in Stockholm: a successful Canadian arts-education export).

Learning Through the Arts has a bold and well-defined ambition: "to transform the goals, culture and methodologies of public education" by integrating performing and visual arts into the teaching of math, science, history, geography and language. Artists and teachers work closely on the curriculum, with teachers receiving training in the ways the arts can be used in various subject areas, and artists getting training in educational principles and classroom dynamics. Schools and teachers choose the arts disciplines they want to work in, then brainstorm with artists to decide how to use those disciplines to meet curriculum expectations in the chosen subjects. Creativity is the watchword. In one workshop, dancers had Grade 5 science students build "structures" by stacking and connecting their own bodies, then devise human "mechanisms" to move their structures into different places and positions. One class used their bodies as a conveyer belt to move their classroom teacher across the length of the gym.

Given the treatment of the arts in Canada's schools, the LTTA program is probably as close to the ideal of curriculum integration as we can currently come. There is not much point in sending out touring theatre troupes and dance ensembles to play to students with no developed awareness of what they are seeing. As John Tusa, the head of London's Barbican Centre, said about his organization's education programs: "Too often I think we are putting down creative mulch on a garden that basically has no plants in it." The LTTA program attempts not only to plant the seed but to induce germination and encourage the plant to flower.

The evidence that the program works is more than anecdotal. A three-year Queen's University study released late in 2002 showed that elementary-school students enrolled in the LTTA program scored up to 11 percentile points higher in math than students without the arts-enhanced classes. More than 6,000 students between the ages of eleven and twelve were tracked for the study, which also showed that children in Grade 6 who were enrolled in the LTTA program were significantly happier to come to school than their peers in non-LTTA schools. In addition, increasing numbers of teachers in LTTA schools feel the arts are an effective way to teach math, science and language and to reach hard-to-educate students, and nearly 90 per cent of all parents in the study said the arts motivate their children to learn. What the study showed, said co-leader Dr. Rena Upitis, is that "time for the arts in school does not come at the expense of achievement in language and math. In fact, we have evidence that the arts may help children do better in math, possibly because they are more engaged in school when arts are part of the curriculum."

The Royal Conservatory of Music may be one of the world's great music schools, but it is also a powerful agent for personal and social change. We change lives by providing a means for self-exploration, creative thinking and problem solving through our music and arts programs. We build the dreams that we share as Canadians for a society in which all people achieve their full potential.

—PETER C. SIMON, president, RCM

If Learning Through the Arts does nothing more than help children and teenagers cope with the emotional challenges they face, as it has already done for these young people, it will surpass any expectations anyone could have for its success.

—DR. JOYCE WILKINSON of the Ontario Institute for
Studies in Education, University of Toronto, and head of the Learning
Through the Arts Toronto assessment team

The ArtSmarts story is an example of what can happen when people decide to take education into their own hands. In 1998, the J.W. McConnell Family Foundation committed $5 million over five years to a scheme designed to put artists and the arts into schools and communities. "We created ArtSmarts to bring the arts back into the curriculum of Canada's public schools because we think creativity is critical to the future of education and the economy," says Tim Brodhead, president and CEO of the foundation. With the Canadian Conference of the Arts as the organizing secretariat, ArtSmarts works with ten partners across Canada, ranging from arts organizations to local foundations to school boards, each of which creates programs according to the specific needs of its community.

The idea is hardly new; artists have worked within the school walls for years. But the range and effect of the ArtSmarts programs are remarkable, because, like the Royal Conservatory's Learning Through the Arts program, ArtSmarts aims for something much greater and ultimately more enriching than merely exposing students to the arts: to integrate the arts with the basic school curriculum. Music, for instance, might be used to help students understand mathematical concepts, sculpting to teach geography, painting to interest children in recording local history. In its first five years, ArtSmarts engaged more than 185,000 young people, 2,800 artists, 5,000 educators and community members and 500 volunteers across Canada, and late in 2003 Brodhead announced a further investment of $4.6 million to expand the program.

Does it work? Dr. Kit Grauer, a professor in the Curriculum Studies Department of the University of British Columbia, is quoted in *The ArtSmarts Story* as saying she believes the impact on students is profound, though difficult to quantify. Results might not show up in specific tests; rather, the cognitive gains come through a new understanding of, say, multiculturalism or the environment: "major attitudinal changes ... really deep, thoughtful things." Certainly, ArtSmarts themes—carefully chosen to cover the requirements of each of the provincial curricula—tend to deal with the big, global issues such as the environment, human rights and democracy. They have helped combat racism and bigotry by exposing students to world cultures. The emphasis is always on programs that grow out of the needs and concerns of the community in which they are presented. Each is tailored to the individual circumstance. As Kit Grauer puts it, they are designed to generate an understanding of "who you are, and where you are in the world."

At Whiteshell Provincial Park in Manitoba there are "boulder mosaics" in the shapes of snakes, turtles, fish, wolves and other animals. These are petroglyphs, created by aboriginal people centuries ago.

Most of the students in Grades Two and Three at North Memorial School in Portage La Prairie are aboriginal or Metis. Working with artist Carmen Hathaway, they are gluing several varieties of Manitoba-grown beans to painted styrofoam food trays, recreating the petroglyph patterns which were first imagined by their distant ancestors. Manitoba produces nearly forty per cent of Canada's bean crop and exports to 39 countries around the world, and a local company has contributed these beans.

Several of these students, mainly boys, says teacher Val Smith, are "rushers" who don't listen well, can't focus, don't concentrate. But this project has changed them. Here and elsewhere, the children who do well in arts projects are often the ones who do not learn well from traditional classroom routines. This is hardly surprising, since research on learning styles shows that only about twenty per cent of us learn best from reading and listening as opposed to active participation.

> —from *The Artsmarts Story*, by SILVER DONALD CAMERON,
> published by the Canadian Conference of the Arts

We are almost finished our ArtSmarts program. It has been a wonderful experience. Last week we hosted a Welcome Ceremony at the Big House in Alert Bay for over 300 people. We feasted and danced. One exciting thing was that our first dance of the ceremony was the Paddle Entrance Song. This was a previously lost song that was rediscovered three years ago on old recordings. Through our ArtSmarts program the students learned the words and dance steps to this song. We were the first group to dance this song in many, many years. We were the first group to dance this song in the new Big House. This is an incredible honour for our students, especially since so many people came to witness and record the event. But even better . . . now all 93 of our students can sing this song. It is no longer a lost song . . . but alive!

> —SUSAN PLENSKY, school principal and project
> coordinator, Alert Bay, B.C., May 2002

Another significant arts program is ArtStarts in Schools, which reaches over 500,000 B.C. young people annually, with perform-ances, workshops and special events (many of them linked to Art-Smarts and Learning Through the Arts initiatives) in schools and communities around the province. Calgary Partners in Education Society (CAPES) administers ArtSmarts in Calgary, along with, among other programs, a ground-breaking collaboration with the Calgary Board of Education to deliver ArtsCORE, which explores the idea of arts-infused education in the curriculum.

In Vancouver, Arts Umbrella functions as a visual and performing arts institute for young people, aiming to make arts education accessible to all children, regardless of their financial situation. Since its opening in 1979, with an enrolment of 45 students, Arts Umbrella has grown to reach more than 30,000 young people annually—including 17,000 inner-city school students who take part in the organization's outreach program. More than 3,600 children from low-income neighbourhood schools participate in drama and visual arts workshops at the school itself.

Because of its substantial enrolment, Arts Umbrella was chosen by Heritage Canada in 2002 as the focus for an Ipsos-Reid study designed to measure the impact that involvement with the arts has on students and their families. Among the principal findings: involvement with the arts is considered a means for children to be successful outside the school system; it builds self-esteem and confidence; it develops both the mind and the focus of the child; and it helps develop self-discipline and motivates independent thinking. Ninety per cent of students interviewed, both past and current, said arts exposure had had a positive impact on them, and 86 per cent of alumni were still involved with the arts in some way. "While many of the students who participated will not likely pursue a career which is directly related to the arts," said the report, "both parents and students are confident that the skills gained through arts education will contribute to their overall success, no matter what their career path might be."

One hopeful indicator that change might be in the wind is the fact that educators themselves are less likely these days to need persuading about the value of in-school contact with art. They have read the studies and seen the results. They know that these programs help children explore their creativity, develop critical thinking and communication skills, and gain an awareness of environmental and multicultural issues. When arts experiences are embedded in the structure, rather than superimposed, they also transform the school environment, making it a place of adventure and discovery, building new connections among the students, and often making connections with children who are otherwise disengaged from the educational experience, particularly those who have problems with language skills. "When artists go into the classroom," says Wendy Newman, executive director of ArtStarts in Schools, "the kids recognize that artists don't think or act like parents or teachers, and many kids react positively to that."

> *Students in Smithers, B.C., responded to racist graffiti in their community by erecting a totem pole in front of their school, as a reassurance to all who entered that they were welcome.*

On the Web, meanwhile, schools have access to both Composers in Electronic Residence and Writers in Electronic Residence, interactive sites where students can exchange composition and writing with professional artists. Learning Through the Arts has developed an e-learning component specifically geared to remote communities of Canada. More informally, a lively network of festivals for young people has been built across the country, linking schools to wide-ranging programs of performance, visual arts and literature.

As the Learning Through the Arts program recognizes, it is not enough simply to put artists and teachers in a classroom together, either virtually or in real time. Those who believe the arts and culture have a social relevance often share the view that professional training programs in the arts (and, for that matter, in arts management) should promote an awareness of the artist's relationship with and responsibilities to the community at large, exploring why that relationship is important and how it might be developed. In other words, art for art's sake is no longer sufficient; both teachers and artists need to know how to collaborate in ways most effective for students. Given the increasingly pluralistic nature of Canadian society, an important element of any school arts-education program should also be a focus on intercultural studies as a way to develop a sense of community and cooperation and to learn to be comfortable with permanent change.

The responsibility lies not only with educators. Arts, culture and heritage organizations are paying careful attention to the structure and content of their outreach programs for young audiences. Standing at the door of the local all-purpose theatre complex to welcome busloads of kids to a performance by the ballet or the orchestra is no longer adequate. Top-down does not work. Instead, organizations work for inclusion, enlisting students themselves in discussing what they will be exposed to and, equally importantly, encouraging them to articulate reasons for their choices, thus helping them to recognize the significance of the arts in their daily lives.

Arts Education: A Way Forward

TO SHAPE THESE affirmations of the social benefits of arts education into a framework for action, serious thought should be given to the creation of a pan-Canadian task force. This could be formed under the aegis of the Coalition for Arts Education in Canada and bring together governments and educators as well as agencies such as the Canada Council for the Arts and NGOs such as the Canadian Conference of the Arts. Its mandate would be to define the ways in which the arts can be better employed in Canada's schools to develop the skills students will need to thrive in the communication and information age.

Among the issues such a task force might consider are the following:

- Strategies to ensure the integration of all artistic disciplines into the general school curriculum, rather than allowing the arts to be treated as a separate area of learning and experience—for example, making art a learning tool, rather than a learning target.
- The establishment of a sustained pan-Canadian program of arts advocacy, which would affirm and demonstrate—to teachers as well as to parents—the multiple values the creative experience holds for children and spread the word about programs available both inside and outside the basic school curriculum. The framework articulated by the National Symposium on Arts Education could be a useful start.
- The creation of a national awards program for arts educators, along the lines of the Prime Minister's awards for teaching in the sciences, mathematics and technology, and of a parallel national awards system to recognize schools that make exceptional efforts to integrate the arts into the general curriculum and raise the standards of arts education.
- The inclusion of arts training in the general programs of universities and teacher-training faculties, and the provision of a greater range of postgraduate arts courses, field placements and skills upgrading for teachers in the field. In recent years, professional development in arts teaching, and in the use of the arts for teaching other subjects, has become a recognized element of training in some Canadian university faculties of education, but here too much more remains to be achieved.
- The establishment of some form of accreditation for professional artists working in schools, perhaps through the medium of an interfacing agency such as ArtSmarts or ArtStarts, to ensure that quality standards in education are maintained.
- Strategies to encourage private foundations to provide financial support for arts-education initiatives and to encourage Canada's

national arts-education institutions to integrate business aspects of arts activity into their curricula, in order to equip emerging artists with the tools to manage their affairs.

• The affirmation of the regard for excellence as a prerequisite of arts activity within the education system. The attitude that, for instance, theatre for young audiences is somehow inferior to theatre for adults remains widespread. It must be a point of principle not to foist substandard productions onto unsuspecting school audiences.

• The creation within the federal Canada On-Line Web service network of a site where artists and teachers could make contact, exchange ideas, learn about each other's disciplines, and collaborate on bringing involvement with the arts into the nation's schools.

One of the most frequently cited difficulties in turning the dream of universal student access to the arts into practice is the shortage of materials and equipment. Practically, it is time to establish a system whereby the federal government sets aside funds to reinforce arts education across the country. Parameters for access to these funds can be set deliberately wide; a community centre or art gallery might make a request for materials for an art-making class; individual schools or school boards might ask for help to augment the arts education already funded by the provinces, perhaps in the form of artist visits or studio field trips. The effect would be the same: to give young people access to practical experiences of art and art-making. And such an approach would exist outside the traditional areas of arts support, with their necessary apparatus of juries and assessed quality.

We might wish also to study the experience of Holland, where students are given vouchers covering admission costs to arts events that they choose themselves and "cultural youth passports" that allow them discounted admission to a wide variety of other arts events. This would have a double impact: students would have the impetus to make informed choices, and arts organizations would be spurred into expanding their youth-oriented programming.

A new stress could also be placed on the distribution of work by young creators, not only through the programs of the Canada Council for the Arts—which of necessity have a condition of artistic excellence attached—but through the communications medium of choice for the majority of young Canadians, the Internet. And not only distribution, but celebration. Awards, prizes, showcases and festivals are all effective ways to display and honour—and thus legitimize—youthful creativity.

Linked to this whole question of education is the marginalization of the liberal arts and humanities in Canada's schools and universities. We find ourselves in an age when the education system—even the higher education system—seems to train its focus primarily on the creation of individuals who can function efficiently in the modern world, rather than bringing any critical sense to bear on the way the world functions. This may have happened for understandable reasons, prime among them our society's obsession with short-term benefits, measurables, deliverables and all the other paraphernalia of the marketplace economy. In the face of those pressures, what price the emotional and spiritual life, what price the pursuit of reason and balance (other, that is, than the balance found in the economic books), what price Northrop Frye's belief that a liberal arts education will give an individual the language to deal with the fragmentation and foolishness of modern life?

This approach is selling short the country's future. Canada's schools and universities continue to produce graduates more suited to be managers than to be leaders. Public debate lacks spine and complexity. We lack the subtlety of vision, dialogue and reflection that engagement with the great ideas of the past engenders, yet that engagement is necessary if we wish to come to terms with the great challenges of tomorrow.

The business school at the University of Western Ontario has for several years involved the Second City theatre company in improvisational theatre workshops. The adaptability, spontaneity and quick thinking that improv theatre requires is recognized as an invaluable tool, preparing individuals for the unpredictability of the real world of business.

The poet and critic Matthew Arnold believed that art was a tool for society's moral improvement. He saw culture as a storehouse of humankind's noblest spiritual and intellectual aspirations: "the best that has been thought and said in the world." His idealistic Victorian social rectitude is out of fashion these days, but the humanist basis on which his thinking is built (the thought that art addresses our most profound concerns and improves us by exposing us to the highest levels of thought and morality) remains valid. Art does have the power to change us and to comfort us with the recognition of human potential. This was one of art's chief virtues for the Victorians, who saw it as a bulwark against the social challenges of the Industrial Revolution. Art, the manmade answer, stepped in where religion, in the face of commerce and science, had faltered.

If that was so then, how much more tempting to take that approach again. In a world of shifting values and electronic shadows, we need an anchor that says we count. There is also the by no means negligible value of art's handmade values in a technological world, even if these are no more commercially viable than the labour-intensive works of Crispin Elsted, who produces exquisite printing in tiny runs on ancient hand presses in a bucolic corner of British Columbia's Fraser Valley.

The restoration of the liberal arts to the mainstream of education is crucial to the healthy development of Canada's culture, now more than ever, when technological and market forces dominate the national and international agendas. There is more to life than merchandise and money, more to personal fulfilment than quick advancement and a comfortable salary. The knowledge society is already upon us, with its insistent demands for vision. As a country, we are already heavily committed to the notion of investment in innovation. But knowledge and innovation are not enough; they must be guided by wisdom, by an understanding of moral purpose, by reason, by respect for the other, and by a sense of the greater good.

It follows that equipping Canadians with the tools to understand the moral foundation of liberal thought, through acquaintance with cultural expression, is an obligation to Canada's future. Properly funded, the program of graduate research at the Social Sciences and Humanities Research Council has an important contribution to make in this regard. Some of our universities, recognizing the gap in the services they offer, are tackling the problem at source by offering "foundation years"—obligatory courses in the humanities, sciences and social sciences that introduce the classic debates about social values. Others are beginning to experiment with "service learning"— courses that combine volunteer involvement in the community with academic study. A clear opportunity exists here for the arts and cultural community to link hands with the academy. Innovative programs of student internship with arts organizations could provide young Canadians with invaluable insights into the possibilities of cultural expression and its values for society at large, developing an intensified sense of the opportunities and rewards of responsible citizenship.

Creating "fine-textured human beings"

FOR MORE THAN a dozen years, Vancouver real estate magnate Bob Bentall and his wife, Linda, have been investing their considerable fortune, at the rate of $3 million a year, in their remarkable Ailanthus project. The beneficiaries are at-risk young people plucked from the tough schools and neighbourhoods of the most disadvantaged areas of the city. Many have a history of crime and violence. In return for a zero-tolerance, no-drugs, no-piercing, no-bad-language commitment to take the program seriously, Ailanthus fully funds their education. The intake of students is about 175 a year, and students are supported from the age of twelve until graduation; in many cases, graduation from college or university. The central facility cost $8 million to build, and a $2-million residence is available for the most threatened participants. The aim of the program is to turn young lives around and offer a fresh chance, through hard, committed work, to achieve academic, personal and social success. A key element—"the glue that holds it together," in the words of Linda Bentall, "and an amazing tool for their social development"—is the performing-arts segment of the school. A combination of music, dance, aerobatics and martial arts, it uses the training framework of Le Cirque du Soleil as a model, helping to build discipline, teamwork and personal confidence in the participants: helping to create what Linda Bentall calls "fine-textured human beings."

THE INTEGRATION OF ARTS activity into programs to fight youth crime and other social problems is winning increasing recognition. The Ailanthus program is a high-profile, big-budget example of the kind of work with at-risk youth that is going on in many cities in Canada. It is also a demonstration of the practical, life-changing contribution that socially responsible business can make.

In Winnipeg, the International Children's Festival has provided a creative alternative to criminal and anti-social behaviour for inner-city youth with a performing-arts program that lets the young people develop skills as instructors and mentors while continuing to develop their own performance skills. In the same city, Manitoba Theatre for Young People took its project on bullying to 3,000 elementary-school children in ten northern Manitoba communities. Based on children's own experiences, the project portrayed the problems of bullying on the playground, allowing children to examine the root causes and explore positive, non-violent ways to handle them. Powerhouse Winnipeg's Village Youth Art Centre project encouraged participants to express themselves through art as a means of overcoming isolation and loneliness, reducing criminal behaviour patterns, and building self-identity and self-confidence. The Metis Resource Centre worked to increase awareness of important Metis historical events and improve language skills through the creation of a colouring book and a historical calendar distributed to the community at large.

In Canada as in Britain and other countries, a wide range of creative partnerships lets young people in problem areas work with groups involved in culture and the arts. And the benefits go far beyond the stimulation of the creative act. These projects can give young people an alternative to burglary, vandalism and violence, and help them learn to make choices, take risks and take responsibility—in essence, to access their own humanity.

Does this approach work? Figures are hard to come by, though studies are underway. In Britain, however, the crime rate in areas where the Youth Justice Board staged similar projects in the summer of 2000 fell by 6 per cent compared with a national rise of almost 4 per cent; criminal damage was down by 14 per cent and domestic burglary by 27 per cent.

It is certainly possible to measure the effect in broad social terms of a work like *ICE: Beyond Cool,* a music-theatre-dance concoction from Vancouver's DanceArts on the theme of teen suicide. *ICE* was built largely on the contributions of teenagers themselves, and it played across Canada not in theatres but in places where teens congregate, such as shopping malls and schools. The production turned out to be not only theatre as social message but also theatre as therapy, vivid affirmation of the life-changing effects and the value of the metaphorical examination of issues that art can uniquely offer.

I cried in almost every scene ... I think the reason I cry is because this show depicts my life almost exactly! On Friday October 3 I tried to kill myself by overdose, obviously it didn't work! The day after, I saw your first public show, and I don't know what happened but your show completely changed my life. It brought me out of my depression, and for that I am very thankful!

— A letter from a teenager received by DanceArts
after a performance of *ICE: Beyond Cool*

None of this is far removed from the idea of art as a healing tool. A choir of Montreal homeless people, many of them alcoholics and former drug addicts, was disbanded after 1,000 performances because many of its members, more stable and more self-reliant as a result of working and travelling with the choir, had found jobs and wanted to move on with their lives. In some North American aboriginal communities, a return to traditional practices and values is helping youth come to terms with alcoholism and drug abuse, and suicide rates are dropping in societies with higher cultural self-esteem. Cree artist Jim Poitras credits his decision at the age of forty to explore his First Nations cultural heritage with saving him from a life of drugs and alcohol. Today his paintings hang in collections in Canada and Europe. *Transformation,* a play he wrote about his life, has been produced with great success in Canada, Germany and Austria, and he travels extensively to teach native dance and music.

Even experimental art has spinoff benefits. David Rokeby's investigations of the way computer technology can use video art are also used to help people with disabilities deal with barriers to communication and mobility. His *Very Nervous System* integrates video cameras, image processors, computers, synthesizers and a sound system to create a space in which the movements of the body itself create sound and music. In Newfoundland, artist Lori Clarke and others have been exploring the interaction between art and medicine. *Breathe,* a collaboration between Clarke and the staff and students at the medical school of Memorial University, combines video, sound, a set and live performance in its explorations of biological, psychological and social issues. "In art as in medicine, a creative force is unleashed when prac-tice leaps beyond the disciplinary and into highly complex human ter-rain," says Clarke. "There is a healing power in this creative process which enters the realm of the poetic."

Recent studies have shown that participation in the arts reduces stress levels; reduces fear and the sense of isolation; has beneficial effects on the immune system; reduces the need for medication and painkillers; and shortens hospital stays. Even itinerant theatre has its role to play: one hospital study in England showed that two-thirds of patients, staff and visitors who experienced live theatrical perfor-mances felt their worries diminish, their stress levels drop and their moods improve. The *British Medical Journal*'s editor, Richard Smith, recently went so far as to suggest that 0.5 per cent of Britain's £50-bil-lion ($130-billion) health care budget be diverted to the arts.

"More and more of life's processes and difficulties—birth, death, sexuality, ageing, unhappiness, tiredness, loneliness, perceived imper-fections in our bodies—are being medicalised," he wrote. "Medicine cannot solve these problems. It can sometimes help—but often at a substantial cost ... Worst of all, people are diverted from what may be much better ways to adjust to their problems. This may be where the arts can help." Predictably, his suggestion—which would put an extra £250 million ($650 million) into arts coffers—was welcomed enthu-siastically by arts advocates. "The arts enable us to live better, to extend our emotional range," said Sir Brian McMaster, director of the Edinburgh International Festival and former director of the Vancouver Opera. "They go to the heart of a lot of psychological illness, by con-structively filling our time. Illness comes in when there is a gap in one's life."

Other evidence shows that attitudes to people with disabilities, individuals who are often marginalized in society, can be changed through exposure to art made by artists and performers with disabil-ities themselves—both through allowing the disability community to assert a sense of cultural pride and identity and by demonstrating what all human individuals have in common.

The arts also have a role to play in the area of corrections. Numerous studies show the positive effect on offenders of involvement with art. In the U.K., about 30 per cent of male prisoners and 40 per cent of female prisoners attend arts classes and, according to the National Campaign for the Arts, violent incidents in jails with arts programs are 60 to 90 per cent lower than in those without. A museum in England devoted to law, justice and punishment recently won the first £100,000 Gulbenkian Prize for Museums for its innovative outreach programs. Nottingham's Galleries of Justice, a museum housed in the old county jail and courthouse, uses its materials as the basis for courses intended to turn wayward youth away from crime and drug abuse—with such success that juvenile courts instruct young offenders to participate. Along with its more general public programs, which feature actors as prisoners and jailers in the old cells and courtrooms, the museum collaborates with social workers and police to offer a range of courses for young offenders and at-risk youth. Montreal's Cirque du Soleil holds workshops with street kids to help them build self-esteem. As Harry Thomas, director of the Seattle Housing Authority, puts it: "When children express themselves through dance they may no longer need a broken window, or the power of their voices, a can of spray paint, or a gun to make their point."

Just as artistic activity gives young people a means of self-expression and self-understanding, similar forces seem to operate on prison inmates. In his TV series and subsequent book *The Language of Life,* U.S. broadcaster Bill Moyers profiled Jimmy Santiago Baca, a violent inmate who began to write poetry while in a maximum security prison in Arizona. Baca, whose poetry has since been published widely and has won awards, claimed poetry saved his life. He once attempted to read his poems at a parole board hearing. "It was my only way," he told Moyers, "of telling them this is who I'd become—this is who I am, this is my record." B.C. writer Ed Griffin, who has taught for several years at Matsqui Institution, believes creative writing can help rehabilitate prisoners. "They start off with a screw-the-system attitude. But then they start writing about their childhoods and they begin to realize all kinds of things. It's a process of learning and of increasing self-awareness."

3

THE PROMISE
OF OUR DIVERSITY

Canada is defined by far more than its political boundaries or economic relationships. In these times of rapid change and globalization, it is more important than ever that we know who we are as Canadians and what brings us together.

— Governor General ADRIENNE CLARKSON,
Speech from the Throne, January 2001

THROUGHOUT MUCH OF the twentieth century, we shaped our attitudes to culture in Canada largely according to European traditions. Our principal arts funding agency, the Canada Council for the Arts, drew on the English model for both its structure and its decision-making processes, and assessments of excellence were in great measure made according to established European standards.

The European creative canon is a rich and honourable one, and as long as modern Canada clung to its European origins as a means of defining, inspiring and entertaining itself, it was logical that we should look to that canon for definitions of excellence. Our orchestras, theatres, dance troupes and opera companies all emphasized the European heritage in what they offered to their audiences. Even when we began to develop our own strong stables of creative artists in these disciplines, those artists mostly worked in the established European styles. While the accent was Canadian, and so increasingly were the themes, the form was traditional, and the tradition came from Europe.

Long before the turn of the millennium, however, it was clear that we were living in a vastly changed world. The aboriginal presence in our nation, so long pushed to one side, was at last commanding proper respect and consideration. And immigration was bringing permanent change to the face of Canada. Today, close to 200 languages (including more than 50 aboriginal languages) are spoken every day in Canada. Per capita, Canada receives more immigrants each year than any other country in the world. By 2016, according to census projections, one in five Canadians will be of non-European origin, double the number recorded in 1991. The main streets of our cities are polyglot hubs of cultural activity, where a Thai restaurant exists side by side with an Iranian grocery and a Korean smoke shop. Modern urban culture in Canada, as in many other countries, is a fluid cosmopolitanism, endlessly reinventing itself; influence and effect in ceaseless mutation. Europe has been challenged; it is now one element among many.

What we make of Canada in the century to come will depend on how we as a society relate to these new cultural demographics. The imminent retirement of the baby boom generation, which will hit its peak in about 2015, and the steady growth of the Canadian economy will bring about a demand for skilled individuals that will far outstrip the trained-in-Canada response. Canada will increasingly look abroad for talent to fill the vacuum in the sectors that sustain our economy. Teachers, doctors, nurses and information technology workers comprise only a few of the occupations where demand exceeds (or will soon exceed) supply. But Canada faces growing competition for the best and brightest minds of the developing economies—not only from those economies themselves, which are going out of their way to retain their graduates, but from other countries that have recognized the looming challenge. The federal government has recently taken steps to increase ease of access for qualified immigrants and has set its target immigration level at 1 per cent of the Canadian population—about 300,000 people—every year.

The pressures such massive demographic changes put on society, and the clashes of views that they engender, demand great resources of mutual understanding if Canada is not to decline into a balkanized confederation of minority groups and interests. The challenge that contemporary societies face is to retain their specific character, individuality, principles and beliefs. It is a problem of which Canada has long been aware; it lies at the heart of the enduring debate about multiculturalism and cultural diversity.

Canada must now preserve its identity by having many identities.

—NORTHROP FRYE

Pluralism and cooperation are the foundation on which Canada was built and the core of its social strength today. Founded by two peoples, built as an open society of many cultures, Canada is as much a social invention as a nation-state: not the melting-pot of the United States, but a unified society built on recognition of the fundamental integrity of parallel ethnicities and beliefs. Out of this has come Canada's international reputation for flexibility, reconciliation and accommodation. It was a Canadian who drafted the Universal Declaration of Human Rights. It was neutral Canada that was chosen by India and Pakistan as the place where they could play their fiercely contested international cricket matches in safety. It has even been argued that there is a way of writing that is distinctively Canadian. "It is typical in Canadian literature," says Yann Martel, author of *The Life of Pi,* "to have a multicultural element, to have no strong centralized version of things, to find less posturing than you might find in American literature."

Out of this, too, has come Canada's recognition that every citizen has rights (including the right, for instance, to take advantage of the entrepreneurial opportunities of the new order) and every citizen has responsibilities (for instance, to contribute to the provision of mutual care). Citizenship and inclusion in this society carry with them the obligation to strive to ensure implementation and protection of these rights. They should also include entitlement to full participation in the world of imagination and creativity.

Very few things turn on the kids like [world music] does. What we are really doing is promoting an understanding of the diversity that we have. There are lots of prejudices that are established out of ignorance. This is one way to deal with that ignorance. If we can eliminate prejudicial thought at that level, then we've made a major accomplishment.

— SAL FERRERAS, musician and head of the world music
program at Vancouver Community College

It is in this area of pluralistic living—the art of being good and civil neighbours—that Canada has a leadership role to play. The individual sense of identity and self-worth developed through creative activity will be ever more necessary as the conformist pressures of globalization intensify. And it is through engagement with culture, in its broadest definition, that we will begin to understand the implications of such momentous change. Art gives us the metaphors that allow us to come to grips with epochal concepts at human scale. And it lets us know our neighbours better.

If we are to fulfil our potential as messengers of social change, all segments of Canadian society must participate. Cultural diversity is as important within national borders as outside them. Traditional forms of expression (the music of Cape Breton Island, the carvings of

Canada's Inuit, the taiko drumming of Vancouver's Japanese community) as well as the manifestations of the new cultural hybridity (the
"jazz butoh" fusion of styles presented by Vancouver's Kokoro Dance;
the dub poetry of Toronto's Caribbean community; *Beatrice Chancy,*
the opera based on black slavery in Nova Scotia; Cree playwright
Floyd Favel's use of a Siberian historical incident as inspiration for a
play that addresses Canadian aboriginal concerns) are all elements of
what we think of as the culture of Canada.

*Leave the windows of your house open and let the breezes blow through
in all directions, but let the foundations of your house be solid and
unshakeable.* —MAHATMA GANDHI

In light of the multiple challenges to modern nationhood—not
only the challenges presented by globalization and the multinational
corporation, but the challenges implicit in human progress, among
them the growing digital divide, the threats to the environment, an
unstable global peace, the crises in health and education—it becomes
ever more important to encourage human interaction and understanding. Some commentators have gone so far as to call for an entirely
new cultural contract, favouring cultural pluralism over cultural con-
formity and promoting cultural cross-fertilization as a means to bridge
the yawning gaps that separate so many modern citizens from one
another.

In Canada, the foundations for such a contract are firmly in place:
participation, representation, the rule of law, the protection of freedoms, all on the basis of simple citizenship. We now need to build on
that foundation to protect the diversity of human beings and articulate a system of ethics that goes beyond the administration of law to
embrace the ideas of generosity, mutual care and the common good.
The political force of our time will be individual participation in this
great debate. No one interested in shaping a world for the well-being

of all humanity will be able to sit on the sidelines. Momentous decision-making must occur, and individual involvement will be essential.

We already see shifts in this direction. As the world lurches from crisis to crisis, compassionate reflection on the human condition helps strengthen interest in humanitarianism and environmental action. It is a movement no longer limited by national borders. At a time when we can share views and canvass opinion anywhere in the world (a phenomenon made possible by the same communications and information technologies that have helped consolidate the new world economic order), independent transnational networks of concerned individuals gain voice and strength.

This might be seen as a threat to national societies, in that these evolving transborder connections have the potential to create global solidarities stronger than nations themselves. In a similar way, we might fear that globalization, in its imposition of a universal cultural diet, will bring about a kind of cultural cleansing, in which difference is wiped away, the colours of our world are made uniform, and we are in effect de-cultured.

On the other hand, we might welcome globalization as a positive force in breaking down barriers between cultures and stimulating the interaction of language and interests. If we find ourselves tempted to agree with Samuel Huntingdon's 1993 assertion that "the clash of civilizations will dominate global politics" (and, a decade on, he seems to have had his finger on something), we would be wise to do what we can to encourage understanding among those civilizations. And we might welcome the communications revolution as a means to help us manage that.

In South Africa, the Moving Into Dance Mophatong company has attracted thousands of young people to its programs integrating dance and education. Vancouver choreographer Joe Laughlin, artistic director of the dance company Joe Ink, joined forces with the racially integrated Mophatong to create a Canada-Africa collaborative production specifically for young audiences. Every Body/Sonke Sisonke, *described as "one part tribal village dance, one part gymnastics-inspired contemporary Western movement," received its world premiere in South Africa in the fall of 2001 and its Canadian premiere at the Vancouver International Children's Festival the following spring. Laughlin, a former competitive gymnast who has worked extensively with young audiences, said the collaboration celebrated "physical and cultural diversity. African culture is interdisciplinary, and there is a cultural history of singing and dancing for everyone. This would become the structure for our piece."*

In recent years, Canada has been actively involved in an international movement to reinforce the sacrosanct nature of cultural diversity—in simple terms, the idea that the uniqueness and plurality of cultures is as important to humanity as biodiversity is to nature, and that cultural expression should be regarded as a good not subject to the laws of the marketplace and significantly different from other types of product. The drive to establish an international agreement on cultural diversity has been characterized in some quarters as a form of cultural protectionism, equivalent to the tariffs and import restrictions that are integral to international trade. But far from being a defensive posture, as many suggest, its effect would be to advance the healthy development and expression of each society's individual cultural strengths. Under the levelling influence of globalization, a nation's cultural heartbeat becomes its source of pride and identity, and an international agreement on the unique importance of cultural diversity can help ensure that a nation's cultural expression is given its own space in which to grow.

A society built on diversity develops its own system of mutual support; members with differing backgrounds and life experiences bring a variety of skills and knowledge to the mix, giving the overall society greater resilience and durability. Diversity of creative expression gives us all a sense of the wildly varied mix of stimuli and tradition that our society can build on. Each time a species becomes extinct—tree, plant, bird, mammal, reptile, insect—we are poorer, our world less complex and rich. In the same way, each time we allow a form of cultural expression to shrivel, we deprive ourselves of the chance to learn and grow. Protection of diversity encourages flexible thinking and a more agile response to challenge. It also promotes a more civil society.

The action plan that came out of the International Conference on Cultural Policies for Development in Stockholm in 1998—a conference in which Canada established a clear leadership role—had these objectives: to make cultural policy a key component of development strategy and to promote the integration of cultural policies alongside social and economic policies, in recognition that culture—the free expression of a nation—and democracy are inextricably linked.

This clearly goes beyond sending our ballet companies and our writers as an advance corps to polish Canada's image in nations with whom we want to establish trade. Culture has the ability to change attitudes, to foster the mutual respect that will help ensure a more peaceful world. Show someone the way another culture uses music or theatre or dance or words as a form of self-expression, and understanding grows; with understanding comes compassion, and respect develops. The likelihood of conflict is that much diminished.

Today, more than ever, to modify the words of John Donne, no nation is an island, entire unto itself. In our wired world, it is impossible to thrive in isolation. The old walls have fallen; frontiers are more and more seen as constructs of the imagination. Practically, a recognition of cultural diversity can help develop a sense of involvement within local communities. It can spark new ideas of ways to live together and help protect against the stresses that occur when cultures brush up against each other. Confidence and security in our individual cultural identities provides a bulwark against xenophobia, giving us the resilience and adaptability to go on reinventing ourselves. We can integrate ourselves into a new society, involve ourselves in its affairs and contribute to its development, without having to sacrifice what it is that has made us who we are.

Maiko Bae Yamamoto and five fellow students at Simon Fraser University were so frustrated with the lack of diversity on the local arts scene they formed the Boca Del Lupo theatre company after graduating from university in 1998. A six-member troupe whose members range from Japanese / Korean-Canadian to Irish-Canadian, Boca Del Lupo aims to promote cultural diversity by sharing personal experiences of ethnicity— a mandate that arose from Yamamoto's discouraged view of the market for ethnic actors. — PETER BIRNIE, *Vancouver Sun*, April 14, 2001

It is important to remain clear-eyed about this process. Mingling cultures is not easy. Not everything about multiracial Canada is harmonious. Frictions still occur. The history of Canada's treatment of its aboriginal peoples is checkered, and understanding and justice can still be in short supply, as Alanis Obamsawin made clear in her documentary on the clash between the colonizing powers and the Mi'kmaq, *Is the Crown at War with Us?* Pico Iyer reminds us that "Every time two worlds cross, a spark of uncertainty and fear rises up between them, something visceral and primal that comes with a scent of danger." And it would be wishful thinking to suggest that Canada is free of intercultural suspicion, intolerance or outright racism. This does not mean that we cannot find common ground across cultures. Rather, by recognizing, sharing and understanding our cultural variations, we are less fragmented and divided.

As a nation we define ourselves by our complexity, and we should resist all attempts to homogenize and simplify. Ideally, what will emerge is a cosmopolitan community of artists whose affiliations go beyond the confines of race or culture, creating freely from all the materials society offers. The voices of the so-called minority cultures of Canada can be loud and exuberant in their determination to assert their historical difference from the rest of Canada and in their pride at being part of the new society we are making together. Approaching difference in a spirit of celebration (poet Lillian Allen calls it "letting go of the rigidity of sameness") has not been easy, but if anyone can do it, the cultural community can. Its members know what it feels to be marginalized.

In Mina Shum's movie *Long Life, Happiness and Prosperity*, Vancouver seems to be entirely populated by Chinese people. Deepa Mehta's movie musical, *Bollywood/Hollywood*, transfers Indian culture to Toronto and, in the process, turns Toronto into a city populated by Indian people, a city in which Hindi songs exist side by side with the poetry of Pablo Neruda and quotations from Shakespeare. Mehta believes Canada has moved beyond multiculturalism into a period of *global* culture. If this is so, all the more reason to equip Canadians with the tools to make the most of this remarkable opportunity. At the very least, exposure of this kind to our cultural diversity can provide the spur for each of us to suspend our deeply rooted beliefs and engage in an open way with the unfamiliar.

> *Identity is local and regional, rooted in the imagination and in works of culture; unity is national in reference, international in perspective and rooted in politics ... Real unity tolerates dissent and rejoices in variety of outlook and tradition.* —NORTHROP FRYE, *The Bush Garden*

Ultimately, the value of cultural diversity lies in what it promises for the future. The astonishing sonic fusion that we call world music— fado crossed with klezmer, rap-inflected Arab music, Polynesian rhythms blended into African song, all the heady mixtures we can hear at popular music festivals across the land—is one of the clearest demonstrations of the power that cultural cross-inspiration can have on how we express ourselves. In this world of creativity and imagination, we can find new structures of inclusion, new understandings of the other, new ways to access the tools that will allow everyone to take part. In that regard, as well as many others, the arts and culture are inextricably intertwined with all the other aspects of our lives.

The uniqueness of a people can be invisible to those who know it only as an everyday thing. We do not always see, from within, the extent to which the things that we make are intimate reflections of us, of a local way of doing things, of thinking and feeling and interpreting.
— Australian playwright DAVID MALOUF

My People Will Sleep for One Hundred Years

IN THE CENTURY SINCE the shameful systematic attacks that came close to eliminating Canada's aboriginal cultures, the native peoples of the country have brought about a wholesale revival of their heritage. And it is their artists—Metis, First Nations and Inuit—who have led the movement to restore and re-establish the significance of cultural activity within their communities.

My people will sleep for one hundred years, but when they awake, it will be the artists who give them their spirit back. — Metis leader LOUIS RIEL

Aboriginal artistic expression is rooted in the community experience: in the passing on of knowledge and tradition, the celebration of spirituality and ritual, the ceremonial passages of lives and the marking of place, the expression of both community and individual identity through connections with the animal and cosmological worlds. Through song, dance, carving and painting, artistic expression is integral to the community's connections to its past, its expression of its present and its vision of its future.

However, while traditional knowledge is its foundation, and tradition itself remains revered, much contemporary aboriginal creativity is an imaginative blend in which the historical is infused by the new. In that sense, it has much in common with artistic activity in any culture. All art is protean; it reshapes itself according to the forces of the time. And a growing number of aboriginal artists have begun to experiment with ways in which their traditions can absorb or be adapted to the influences of other cultures.

In 1992, actress Margo Kane established Full Circle: First Nations Performance to give aboriginal artists a chance to cross-pollinate traditional aboriginal performance with modern mainstream theatre. Individuals involved in those experiments have carried the word about the creative potential of this cultural crossover to the wider aboriginal community. Aboriginal artists use their keen awareness of their heritage as a springboard into visual arts, dance, music, theatre, writing, the media arts, performance art ... In the best sense, they cross-fertilize both traditions and disciplines. The vitality of living culture is nowhere more apparent.

The evidence is all around: in the collaboration among aboriginal writers, visual artists and theatre-makers that resulted in *Copper Thunderbird,* a play by the Montreal group Ondinnok on the life of Ojibway painter Norval Morrisseau; on the awards podium in Cannes with Inuit filmmaker Zacharias Kunuk, whose film *Atanarjuat* (The Fast Runner) was voted best first feature; at the Avataq culture centre in Puvirnituq, Nunavut, where the first world meeting of throat singers brought together more than sixty professionals from different generations and traditions to share techniques and explore new practices; in the 150-plus books by female aboriginal authors published in the past decade by Sandra Laronde's Native Women in the Arts; on the Internet at Nation to Nation's *Cyberpowwow* (www.cyberpowwow. net), a multimedia environment where artists and writers share their work and discuss the influence of technology on aboriginal life; on the stages of the Banff Centre, where the aboriginal dance opera *Bones,* four years in the making, brought together singers, dancers and actors from three continents and six countries; in halls across Saskatchewan where the Saskatchewan Native Theatre Company staged *Love Songs from a War Drum,* an updated Romeo and Juliet story based on real-life stories of love, family and gangs gathered from young participants in healing and talking circles; at a print shop in St. John's, Newfoundland, where Ontario artists Michael Robinson and Newfoundland artist Jerry Evans joined forces in a printmaking project reviving the memory and culture of the Beothuk people.

And it is not only in Canada that aboriginal artists are making their mark. Canadian aboriginal creativity is flourishing internationally: at the Edinburgh Festival, where Winnipeg playwright Ian Ross's play *FareWel* (winner of a Governor General's Literary Award) was a hit with critics and audiences; on the concert circuit in Scandinavia, where Cambridge Bay throat singer Tanya Tagaq Gillis teamed up with Iceland's pop star Bjork; in Australia, where a Sydney aboriginal artists' co-op has collaborated with the Winnipeg artist-run centre Urban Shaman.

The challenge now is to find the best ways to reinforce that flourishing and at the same time strengthen the managerial infrastructure that will give aboriginal cultural expression greater access to all Canadians. More on that later in this book.

Art also serves as a healing tool, as I deal with issues—with world issues that affect all of us, as well as personal ones. People from different backgrounds and experiences can be touched and brought together by art. This is really important to me, as a First Nations person, because of the long tradition of storytelling. —Visual artist GEORGE LITTLECHILD

4

THE POWER OF MYTH:
THE IMPORTANCE OF
OUR STORIES

We haven't got any identity until somebody tells our story.
The fiction makes us real.

—ROBERT KROETSCH

WHEN COMPOSER CHAN KA NIN began researching Chinese-Canadian history in 1989, he found inspiration in two seemingly disparate events: the hammering in of the last spike on the CPR in 1885 and the arrival in B.C. in the 1860s of a group of 265 Chinese migrants—a group that included only one woman. He made the woman the central figure in a tragic love story set against the building of the CPR, and from that evolved the outline of an opera, *Iron Road*.

Of all the art forms, opera is the most expensive to produce, which is one reason why major opera companies tend to favour established works from the traditional repertoire. However, the Toronto production company Tapestry New Opera Works dedicates its efforts to staging contemporary works, and they chose Chan's ambitious cross-cultural vision for production. Tapestry recruited CBC Radio, the Canada Council for the Arts, the Toronto Arts Council and the Ontario Arts Council as co-commissioners, and private donors helped underwrite the $1-million-plus budget. Playwright Mark Brownell and songwriter George K. Wong joined Chan on the creative team. What evolved was a musical story of drama, myth, history and romance—at its heart, the conquering of adversity to build a new life. The story and the production of *Iron Road* were also useful teaching tools, not only about modern opera but about the history of the Chinese in Canada, the building of the CPR and Canada's cultural diversity. Funding from the federal Millennium Partnership Program helped underwrite the *Iron Road* website, which links the production with cultural and historical organizations in Canadian Chinese communities and beyond.

Narrative is the bundle in which we wrap truth, hope, and dread. It is how we explain, how we teach, how we entertain ourselves. It is essential to civilization.

ROBERT FULFORD, cultural commentator,
1999 Massey Lectures

MYTH HAS ALWAYS BEEN a way for peoples to explain their societies, their belief systems, the life they have evolved together. Through shared stories, told among families and passed down the years, history accretes and is made familiar. Truth assumes a comprehensible form. Joseph Campbell called mythology "the song of the universe ... the music of the spheres." He saw mythology as a means for us all to find ways in which our physical life resonates with the eternal and the mysterious: to come to terms with the world of the flesh and the spirit, to understand our place and mark it as our own.

The ancient peoples who lived here before the arrival of the settlers have their own mythologies; so have many of the immigrant peoples who are helping to forge this remarkable country. But Canada itself has little in the way of an authentic mythology—no system of naming the stars, identifying our gods, explaining our origins in ways that transcend the merely scientific. The best we can do by way of mythological heroes lies in the realm of sports or popular music, and even there the crown is often unsteadily worn.

Some have argued that the land of Canada is so immense, so beyond the scale of human endeavour, that any attempt to create a mythology for or from it is doomed to failure. Others counter that the nation's lack of history (a double deficit here: the lack of history that comes with being a newly minted state, and the deliberate erasure of much of the history of our first peoples) means that we are at liberty, as many older nations are not, to create our own mythology, and to go on recreating it until we think we have it right.

Vancouver actor Frannie Sheridan wrote her one-act play The Waltonsteins *in part to come to terms with her family's story. Her parents were Holocaust survivors who emigrated to Canada, where they met and married. But in 1951 a racist attack persuaded her father to change the family's name and faith and deny its Jewish heritage. Sheridan was raised as a Roman Catholic in Ottawa and only discovered the truth about the family when she was nine—and then in conditions of strict secrecy. The play was her way to discover her true identity and to help her family come to terms with its story. "*The* Waltonsteins *is about shame," she has said, "and the damage of being forced to deny one's own identity." The play has toured widely, with members of the Jewish and Catholic communities in Ottawa joining forces to present performances.*

It is to our artists that we turn for help in this continuing attempt to affirm our knowledge of ourselves—through the stories we tell each other, the plays we act, the novels we write, the histories we recount, the fables with which we entertain and instruct each other. Where else do we find such a clear sense of our identity and of our potential as spiritual beings? When we read the books of Lynn Coady or Alistair MacLeod, with their intimate stories of Maritime life, or Wayson Choy's evoca-tion of a childhood in Vancouver's Chinatown in *The Jade Peony*; when we witness the love story that is woven around the building of the transcontinental railway in *Iron Road,* or watch Karen Jamieson's dances built around Haida culture; when we listen to R. Murray Schafer's musical evocations of a northern Canadian landscape or Harry Somers's operatic telling of the tragedy of Louis Riel; when we visit the Haida Gwaii heritage centre in Skidegate or the Head-Smashed-In Buffalo Jump centre near Fort Macleod, we learn each time something about where Canada came from, where Canada is going. The plays of Tomson Highway, Kokoro Dance's butoh-influenced *Rage,* the fiction of Alice Munro: these are all means by which we gain a larger understanding of the community in which we live and a deeper sense of the customs and beliefs that are gathered within our national borders.

It is a cumulative process. To know a people, you must know its history and its beliefs, and this is only possible by degrees. We probe the uneven layers of history one by one, each discovery amplifying what has gone before. But the process makes the idea of a pluralistic Canada comprehensible. The more we know of others' mythologies, the better equipped we are to understand the pressures and possibilities that pluralism can offer. Knowing these stories, having them in our collective memory, gives us ways to understand ourselves.

The written word still defines us. Stories are the R&D of the soul, and the pride Canadians feel in the truths of our history and our achievements is passed from generation to generation fundamentally through the written word. —Publisher SCOTT MCINTYRE

It has been fashionable in some circles to downplay the significance of "the classics" to a generation raised on contemporary pop culture, on the grounds that they are irrelevant to modern ways and modern thinking. But the great themes of art throughout the centuries—politics and power, hubris and the downfall of the great, love and human relationships, treachery and ambition—are enduring, and they amplify many of the concerns that motivate our creators today. From Shakespeare and Molière, the *Oresteia* and the *Ramayana*, *The Dream of the Red Chamber* and the Noh tradition to (a few examples from Canada alone) Robertson Davies and Mordecai Richler, Michel Tremblay and Carol Shields, Atom Egoyan and Zacharias Kunuk, Denys Arcand and François Girard, our mythmakers and storytellers put us in touch with the themes that resonate through our lives. It is through narrative (whether theatrical, literary or visual) that we absorb the metaphors and messages that help us deduce meaning in a bewildering world.

What we need, in the torrent of modern popular culture, is the means to give it all context. Rather than mothball the classics, we must keep them available alongside the current, not as museum artifacts but as what they are: vivid, compelling commentaries on the human condition. It is not a question of either/or, or of qualitative measurement. It is a matter of preserving a balance, offering the context of past insights in a world that is continually striving to seem fresh-made daily.

That balance must include an understanding of the great artistic traditions of all the world's civilizations—Oceania, Asia, Africa, the Indian subcontinent, the Middle East. Many of those traditions inform Canadian society, though much of Canadian society is shamefully ignorant of their significance. If we are to give more than lip service to pluralism, we must integrate these traditions and their modern manifestations into the fabric of modern Canada. Without an openness to both we will surely founder. It is there, surely, in the judicious balance that has evolved between tradition (what one of Canada's cultures would call the wisdom of the elders) and innovation, that the central myth of this land is found.

In an attempt to involve gallery-goers more deeply in the art experience, the Mendel Art Gallery in Saskatoon has introduced the Reading Room, a between-galleries "buffer zone" designed both to give shows context and to allow visitors to record their comments—not only on what they have seen but on anything else related to the world of art. Introduced as a one-year pilot project, the Reading Room was a deliberate attempt to provide an alternative to the traditional "drive-past" method of gallery-going. For the Mendel show on the history of the Qu'Appelle Valley, for instance, which among other things recreated the room of a tuberculosis patient at the Fort Qu'Appelle Sanatorium, a number of contributions to the room's interpretive resources came from members of the public with connections to "Fort San" as well as from individuals who had attended classes there when the sanatorium was closed and the buildings converted to the Saskatchewan Summer School of the Arts. "One of the surprises to us," said programs facilitator Alexandra Stratulat, "is the willingness of people to leave behind what they've made, to add to the gallery displays."

II

MAKING
the CONNECTION

5

THE ARTIST

All art is quite useless.

—OSCAR WILDE

*Art is all about belief, and you've got to want to believe. If you
want to make fun of it, it's very easy to make fun of because all art is
inherently ridiculous ... It's only necessary if you want it to be
necessary ... It's like religion. A belief system.*

—NORMAN ROSENTHAL, exhibitions secretary
at London's Royal Academy

HEN WE TALK of the many benefits that contact with the
arts can bring to society, we must never lose touch with
the fact that art stems from a single source: the artist.
How heroic the act of making art is: a brief attempt to contact other
living creatures, a raised finger of defiance in the face of the inevitable,
a quick stab at immortality before the lights go out. Whether they are
scratching notes onto a music sheet in a studio in the Banff Centre
woods, carving ancient symbols into a weathered log of yellow cedar
on Haida Gwaii, cajoling new movement from dancers in a Winnipeg
rehearsal room, building fanciful structures in a metal shop in
Montreal, manipulating electronic tones on a synthesizer in Halifax or

marrying video with performance in a church hall in St. John's, Canada's artists are the foundation of our cultural expression.

Is art, ultimately, a useless thing, as Wilde playfully suggested? Some would say so. One of its important functions—the function that many would consider the *most* important—is to entertain and divert us, to give us a break from the pressures and privations of the day, to make us laugh, give us comfort, lift our spirits. "Private individual delight and a profound uselessness are fundamental to the nature of all art," according to the English writer Bryan Appleyard. Perhaps he also means art has no value that can be measured, carries out no useful function that a capitalist society would recognize.

Certainly, art makes few Canadian artists rich. Despite the predictable cries of outrage at arts projects that are perceived to be a gross misuse of public money, many of Canada's artists are lucky to live above the poverty line. In 1996 (the most recent year for which figures are available), the average employment income of a visual artist was $12,633. The image of the starving artist living *la vie de Bohème* in a cold-water garret, still a popular romantic notion, is brute reality in many of our towns and cities, and it holds no romance for the individual (and, more likely than not, his or her family) trudging up the narrow stairs to do the starving.

Writer Lynn Coady tells the following story about children's author Sheree Fitch:"She sat at her kitchen table wondering how best to make use of the last $40 in her bank account when, in the nick of time, a children's day camp called. Desperate, Fitch decided to play hardball and informed the camp leader that her usual fee for an appearance was $250 ... The camp leader breezily informed her the fee was no problem, so Fitch packed up her youngest child and off they went ... [After the reading] Fitch practically skipped over to the camp leader and asked to be paid. 'Of course,' the woman smiled back, reaching munificently for her wallet. She extended to the author a $5 bill. She then asked for change. Once Fitch

was able to speak again, and articulate the misunderstanding that had
occurred, the woman's jaw plummeted, her face a rictus of indignation.
'For an hour?' she demanded. 'No,' replied Fitch, doing a slow burn. 'For
17 years.'"

—LYNN COADY, "Will Write for Food," *Vancouver* magazine, October 2001

We have made large strides in our support of the individual creator since Massey-Lévesque. The chances for a professional artist to make a living from the pursuit of his or her vocation are improving. Even so, few artists are ever funded at a level that guarantees them serious security. The success rate for individual artists applying for grants from the Canada Council for the Arts is (depending on the discipline) anywhere from 15 to 25 per cent. In many recent competitions, Canada Council jurors have identified candidates whose work deserves to be funded but who are turned down for lack of resources. Artists are human; they need to eat, clothe themselves, find shelter. How much creative potential has been stifled for lack of the funding to sustain it?

The artists are the ones who oxygenate the blood of the country, and yet all
too often we are perceived as a novelty, to be appreciated but not valued.

—Actor NICOLA CAVENDISH, address to the Vancouver
Board of Trade, November 1994

The hard-nosed argument says we owe our artists nothing. If art is what they choose to do, they must live with the effects of their decision. It is difficult to refute this argument if we are simply concerned with art as a commercial enterprise. But that notion brings us to one of the central problems in this whole vexed matter of public support for artistic activity: our obsession with "value." Value is important, as long as we know what we mean by the term; in our media-dominated society, we often make the mistake of equating it with fame. But value in art has only incidentally to do with popular acclaim. Rather, it has much to do with the ideas the artwork provokes, the questions it raises, the emotional, spiritual and intellectual satisfactions it provides. We engage with the arts because we hope they will provide some direction, meaning, balance and order in a world that all too often seems chaotic. That is one of the reasons we ascribe significance to the things that entertain us. The search for meaning and communality is a basic human need; it dominates our lives. Another reason has to do with our need to escape the pressures of our organized, moment-to-moment, day-to-day lives: to exchange rationality for emotion and imagination.

Reality today is what someone imagined yesterday. —MAVOR MOORE

It is that ability to give us focus, to let us stand above the hurly-burly of the day and take a longer view, that places our artists, our writers and our performers at the forefront of our brave advances towards the future. They engage the great challenges of our race—justice, quality of life, fulfilment of potential—and offer us the fruits of their engagement. We do not have to agree with their conclusions; indeed, the process of disagreeing can sometimes be the best part of learning. But we can generally benefit from giving them our attention. We should be prepared to ensure—both as individual members of the audience, experiencing private pleasure and provocation, and as members of society, which stands to benefit in so many ways from the imaginative activities of our creative community—that they receive fair recompense.

Feel This!

WE ARE STRANGE, contradictory creatures. We welcome—we *expect*—experimentation in science or business or medicine. Pure scientific research is what-if work, essentially speculative in nature, promising no more than the advancement of knowledge. We trust that, even if it has no immediate practical application, it has the potential to be of benefit to society. The accidental discovery of penicillin was one of those benefits. Similarly, anyone in business knows the importance of the R&D department. Not every invention, prototype or patent proves successful, and we understand that we have to fund without guarantee.

Yet we do not extend that same faith to our artists. All too often we throw up our hands in horror when confronted with experiment in the arts. New art makes many of us uncomfortable, particularly when we think we know less about it than we should. We are always looking for the code that opens the safe where the jewels are kept. When I was reviewing opera for the *Vancouver Sun,* people would ask me, as we streamed out of the theatre, to tell them if they liked the performance.

It is a question only the individual can answer, though maybe it is the wrong question to be asking. The wonderful thing about a work of art is that it allows—encourages—as many different opinions as there are individuals who experience it. For many of us, it is enough that we are entertained by the event. But if we want to get more than diversion from our involvement, opinions only go so far. When I was reviewing, the most helpful thing I could tell my readers was not *what* to think about the artwork, but *how.*

Here are some questions it is generally useful to ask: What was the artist trying to tell us? Where does what we have just seen/read/ heard fit into the overall context of the art form? How does it relate to what I know about the world? Was I moved/amused/angered/ provoked/left thoughtful by the experience? Why? Once we start to move in those directions, we give ourselves a chance to get some purchase on the experience. We also give the artist and the artwork their own space.

It is not always that easy, of course. From time to time controversy flares up in the Canadian media about a work of art. One example was Jana Sterbak's *Vanitas: Flesh Dress for an Albino Anorectic* (commonly known as "the meat dress," because Sterbak fashioned 22 kilograms of flank steak into the form of a frock), which addressed the commodification of the female body by fashion and demonstrated the transient nature of all flesh (*vanitas:* all is vanity). The dead rabbits in an artwork by Winnipeg's Diana Thorneycroft provided another. Thorneycroft's *Monstrance* was about our fascination with carnal remains and nature's insistence on returning the body to the earth. The show played on the idea of the religious monstrance, a repository for sacred relics. In the woods around the Manitoba gallery where *Monstrance* was installed, the artist hung rabbit carcasses into which photographic "relics" had been sewn. As putrefaction set in and maggots took over, the relics inside the rabbits became visible. "All of us are moving toward death and dust," Thorneycroft said. "A lot of people won't acknowledge that." Both are works of serious art that addressed significant social issues, but because they addressed the issues in unorthodox ways, what they had to say was outshouted by the sounds of scandal.

As a society, we need to be comfortable, in a way we too often are not, with the fact that art asks difficult questions. There will always be (there *should* always be) scandals. In the words of U.S. dramatist Tony Kushner, "The outrage that is uniquely provoked when subsidized art—especially of course governmentally subsidized art—bites the hand that feeds it, or smears the hand that feeds it with ostensibly-tainted bodily fluids, or places the hand that feeds it up against something horrifyingly unfamiliar and says 'Feel this!' ... That outrage is part of what mustn't be lost, as vital I think as the art that engenders it." Scandals are the sound of society coming to terms with itself, coming to terms with change—change that artists provoke, or at least crystallize, into metaphor, challenging us to think about other possibilities. *Better* possibilities. It is the artist who helps us hope, helps us learn that those better possibilities exist. We need a tolerance for eccentricity.

It would be misguided of us, though, to look to art for answers to the Great Questions. The answers are up to us. Art simply raises the issues, and perhaps offers new ways to think about them. Contemplate the clinically dispassionate photographs that Lynne Cohen makes of ordinary workspaces. She brings to our attention the thoughtless, grim inhumanity of the bleak environments we create, the way we allow industrial design to leach any likelihood of joy even from places meant for pleasure or self-improvement. In these classrooms, spas, laboratories and offices, functionality triumphs over beauty. The spaces are the embodiment of the dehumanized, soulless brave new world. Cohen prescribes no solutions, but she draws our eye, illuminating something important about the way we live.

Art invites us to change our adopted positions, even to cross boundaries. That sometimes makes it disturbing, troublesome, uncomfortable. As humans, yearning for an existence of order and cohesion, we prefer predictability. Anything that can't be quantified, its value measured easily and its intent widely intelligible, becomes, in our rational, organized world, suspect. No wonder we find art disconcerting. It complicates matters, celebrates the stubborn ambiguity of things. As soon as we think we know the code, the artist changes the cyphers. It's like falling in love; the world turns upside down, and nothing is as it was. All we can do is plunge in.

Why did the Taliban bullet down the Buddhas? Why did Hitler burn ooks? Why was Ulysses *banned? Why did Franco refuse to show* Guernica*? Art is potent, confrontational, difficult. It challenges what we are.*
     —JEANETTE WINTERSON, *The Guardian,* November 25, 2002

ARTISTS WILL TELL YOU they will create no matter what response the world gives them, and they will point to many examples of artists who damned the torpedoes and forged ahead, only to die before public awareness of their excellence dawned. Artists create because the act of creation is an instinctive and necessary way for them to make sense of the world. Popular success or acclaim is not the prime consideration.

We have trouble, as a society, with that notion. Since the social revolutions of the 1960s, we have been conditioned by entertainment and the mass media to think that art should be instant in its effect, easily consumable, effortlessly approachable. We are conditioned to assign importance to the popular. Artistic quality is not immaterial to the discussion, but our vision of that, too, is affected by the scale of public enthusiasm. But unless we want everything our artists do to dissolve in an acid bath of personal taste, we must agree, as a society, that there is innate value to art in itself. We may not like it, we may not understand it, but we have to share a belief that there can be intrinsic worth in the works our artists make.

Compounding the problem is the fact that many artists today work outside the boundaries of traditional artistic disciplines. A sound artist might work with the visual arts and have only the vaguest connection with conventional music. Digital art and creation embrace everything from video dance to John Oswald's "plunderphonics." Even conventional notions of acceptability can be a problem. Some sound artists are interested in exploring sound for sound's sake, with no reference to musicality. In an installation by Stéphane Claude and Nancy Tobin, for instance, refrigerators were modified to increase the range and volume of the sound they made, then placed on public display. New art can sometimes seem an insurmountable puzzlement.

The fact that we find some art difficult, however, does not mean that it is exclusionary or (that convenient all-purpose slur) elitist. It may just mean that we need to think harder, look deeper or widen our own range of possibility. Some pieces of art are harder to grasp than others, demanding that we do some work ourselves to get the benefits from them. Unravelling the socio-ethical pros and cons of Jana Sterbak's *Vanitas* is not an easy matter. Works like these can lead us down some challenging byways, both artistic and moral. That doesn't make them deliberately obscure. By branding something "exclusive," we are in effect excluding ourselves.

> *More and more our desire for instant gratification—our need to be kept entertained, whether by literature, pop music or television, without contributing any real effort—is starting to marginalise art of vision, art that questions and may require concentration in order to yield its rewards. Yet it is precisely this art that informs us most about ourselves as human beings. In an ever-changing society we need ever-evolving art to allow us to see our true selves.*
>
> —Composer MICHAEL BERKELEY, *The Guardian*,
> October 26, 2002

NOT EVERY WORK our artists make is going to reach the same level of excellence, of course, any more than everything composed by Mozart's contemporaries was as exalted as the music Mozart wrote. Nor should we automatically bestow our reverence on everything that is new and different and calls itself art. Not all of us would go so far as to echo the comments of the ex-chairman of England's Institute of Contemporary Arts, who asserted (and was promptly fired for doing so) that "most concept art I see now is pretentious, self-indulgent, craftless tat that I wouldn't accept as a gift." But we would do well to bear in mind our awareness that ambition does not always lead to achievement. Many artists can talk a convincing line about what they hope to do with their work; not all of them manage to turn that vision into reality. Our enthusiasm for art must be based in actuality and not in what-might-have-been. Genius, adequacy and mediocrity exist side by side, and it can be a confusing challenge to try to sort them each from each.

One of the reasons modern art gets such consistently bad press is that so many of us try to do that sorting by ourselves. And because most of us do not have the tools, we resort to taste, opinion and gut reaction, and soon enough we start hearing the familiar cries of frustration and self-exclusion. Yet in the long term, whether we think something is good or not good is less important than why—knowing the process that got us to that point, doing the work, putting ourselves in a position to understand. It has to do with our willingness to see through another person's eyes. The artist asks us to look at the world in a different way. The unfamiliar and the unknown always seem like risks; we have to relinquish the controls we have fought hard to establish.

However, in our eagerness to recognize change and innovation, we should never forget that change in itself is a sterile aim. Revolution, by all means; but revolution for a reason. Kicking against the pricks for the sake of novelty will give you nothing but stubbed toes. When we overrun the barricades, let us be sure we have more than upturned applecarts in mind. Beethoven changed the form of the symphony, not for the sake of change but to give himself a more responsive means for emotional and intellectual expression. Jeff Wall and his Vancouver colleagues have changed the way photography is presented and used, not because photography needed to be changed but to express their social concerns more effectively and to investigate theories about the integration of photography and painting.

At the same time, it is in the nature of artistic communication, of all communication, to invite or provoke a response, whether sympathetic or disdainful, interested or angry. An aversion to elitism does not dictate that our artists should dumb down their expectations of what their audiences can handle. We deny art its integrity if we trick it out with false accessibility and easy appeal. We are also misguided if we demand total inclusivity as a criterion for support. By no means is everything for everyone.

We must remember, too, that much of what we regard as the most enduring art was not recognized as valuable during the lifetime of its creator. It is not wise to dismiss the experimental and the avant-garde on the grounds that they interest (or are understood by) only a tiny minority. The visual artist whose works now command some of the highest prices ever paid, Vincent Van Gogh, died penniless and unappreciated. And sometimes the most improbable work can turn out to be broadly transformative. James Joyce's *Ulysses,* the herald of a whole genre of stream-of-consciousness novels, was banned when it first appeared. Conversely, much art that was popular when it was produced fell rapidly into the shadow of neglect, and to base our support or even our interest merely on popularity and acclaim is a dangerous game. Time has a habit of working changes in public taste.

Still, it is crucial that we do not let these arguments for what I suppose is a travelling-hopefully attitude beguile us into any lessening of expectations. In our eagerness to be open to all forms of artistic exploration, we must be careful not to abandon the idea of excellence. To some, the assertion of excellence is a dangerous form of elitism, because it is seen to imply a negative attitude towards the lesser artist or to the preferences of the mass. But even as we recognize that not everything that wins support is going to draw big crowds, even as we stress the need for broader access for all Canadians, excellence must remain the touchstone. The choice of whether or not to attend an event is up to the individual, and that choice will be influenced by many factors, not least among them taste, familiarity, a willingness to try on new things, and—particularly these days—the public image of the event itself. But the excellence of what is offered is a core responsibility.

Take the example of the museum. A museum is an institution designed to provide, for a general public, accessibility to information and reflection, often through vivid displays and interactive facilities. However, it is also concerned with excellence, authenticity, context—

in other words, it is also a centre for serious learning. It might concentrate, in the case of an institution such as the Royal British Columbia Museum, on providing context for an understanding of the development of human society on Canada's West Coast. It might focus, in the case of an institution like the Museum of Civilization, on interpretation of Canadian life in relation to the wider world.

A museum operates, one hopes, to the highest standards of curatorial excellence, but in the best sense, a museum is inclusive, a valuable tool in the process of lifelong learning for every citizen. Knowing more about the creative achievements of our own culture helps us to understand and value the qualities of excellence that made them significant, and at the same time to better understand how other cultures develop. We also (and this is another useful function of a museum) come to recognize how artistic quality—the investment of care and skill in an object's creation—differentiates the aesthetically valuable from the socially significant: the Ming vase from the rough-hewn wooden dish. Artistic merit does not automatically attach itself to a circle of stones that mark an ancient society's worship-ground, although the worship-ground was undeniably significant to that culture.

This is a contentious argument in some circles. The advocates of cultural equivalence, for example, might say that to make a qualitative judgement of this kind implies disrespect. However, it is precisely this ability to discern (discriminate would be a better term, if it did not come freighted with such negative social baggage) that must be encouraged if we wish to develop a proper understanding and appreciation of creative excellence.

We should respect cultural artifacts for their social meaning, whether ritual, ceremonial or religious. But it is misguided anthropological apologism to afford the same level of aesthetic regard to all ancient objects, for not all are created equal. The ability to make that discernment is honed by interaction with cultural history, with all cultural expression. And the ability to recognize excellence—in skill, invention, design, decoration, musical expression—is not the same as cultural snobbery. It is quite the reverse: to be able to identify quality, and to recognize its constituent elements, whatever its origin, allows us to respond with consideration, intelligence and context, rather than ignorance, when we encounter a work of art.

Educating for Uncertainty

IT IS CLEAR THAT WE are not dealing here entirely with the realm of reason. Reason itself, so long the bulwark of progressive thought, has become more and more suspect in recent years. John Ralston Saul, for one, has savaged it severely in a series of elegantly staged attacks. In the world of the arts, reason's status has always been shaky. The demands that science makes for proof, the rigours of logical progression and theorem construction, though necessary for our physical well-being, carry little weight in an area of human experience that deals with the mysteries of the spirit, of the emotions: the illogical and the intuited.

This lack of rootedness in what we think of as the "real" is one cause of society's nervousness about art. Staying abreast means a constant readiness to entertain innovation. Yet it is in the act of liberating us from the surly bonds of reason and allowing us to soar into the blue skies of our collective imagination that art's great value lies.

We need the classics for their links to where we come from, their illumination of the forces that made us, the comfort they give us in the face of adversity, their affirmation of humanity's great truths. But we need new art as well. We may not always like what we see; we may wish we could avert our gaze or even deny that the view is possible (like the South Pacific islanders who, unable to find any reference point in their experience for Cook's passing ships, simply ignored their existence). Ultimately, though, we come to recognize the itch and prod of new art as the signal of the extension of our boundaries.

New art educates us for uncertainty, and it is in uncertainty that we will find the future. Artists, with their clamorous iconoclasm and their strange green hair, are sometimes taken as agents of wilful social anarchy. But their aim is not to destroy the society we live in; their work helps facilitate a manner of thinking that will allow us to create a better one. Artists give us an inkling of a dangerous, exciting irrationality. They give us tools to exercise our intuition. They are messengers from the future.

New work also puts Canadians in touch with aspects of the new world order (or new world *dis*order, as Michael Ames, former head of the Museum of Anthropology at the University of British Columbia, puts it). Work by fifteen artists from Canada and abroad on the theme of displacement and exile made up a 1998 show called *Crossings,* curated by Diana Nemiroff at the National Gallery of Canada. New voices were being heard, and they were questioning the status quo. In her *Group of 67,* for example, Jin-me Yoon, from Korea, offered portraits of Koreans in Vancouver posed against paintings by Lawren Harris and Emily Carr: a new take on what we have come to regard as the classic Canadian landscape. Sometimes, the things these voices have to say create controversy. But they deal with things Canadians need to know.

Art challenges us to reshuffle the composition of our world; it generates an imaginative energy that emboldens us to venture down new paths. We might, for instance, spend a few moments getting in touch with the odd but strangely lulling notions of Montreal's Rober Racine. Racine is a musician, composer, playwright, novelist, visual artist, art critic, essayist, radio producer, performance artist and video maker. He spent fourteen years creating what he termed a "park" of the French language. When the project was installed at the National Gallery of Canada in 2001, it took the form of thousands of little flags inserted in orderly rows in vast blocks of extruded foam. Each flag bore one word cut from the *Petit Robert* dictionary. Mounted around the walls were the dictionary pages, with mirrors behind the spaces from which the words had been cut. Elsewhere music played, scored according to the random appearance of the solfeggio terms *do, re, me,* etc., in the wording of the dictionary definitions. One day, Racine hopes, the entire project will be installed outdoors. The letter K already has been.

In 1978, he performed *Vexations,* a piano piece by Erik Satie, 840 consecutive times in fourteen hours. For another of his projects, *The Salammbô Staircase,* Racine counted the number of words in each of the fifteen chapters of Flaubert's novel *Salammbô* and constructed a wooden stairway, each step representing one chapter and sized according to the number of words (width), sentences (depth) and paragraphs (height) the chapter contained. At the gallery unveiling of this massive piece of lumber in 1980, to mark the centenary of Flaubert's death, Racine read the entire book aloud, mounting the structure chapter by chapter as he did so—it took him fourteen hours—and finally leaping from the topmost level to the gallery floor.

Unusual? Unsettling? Maybe. But let Racine's whimsical ideas play in your head for a while, and you'll find yourself looking at the world in a slightly lopsided way. Racine turns conventional values on their ear, or, rather, suggests that what convention considers important is not the only source of significance. If only for an hour or so, the film of conventionality that clouds our eyes is wiped away. For a while, everything is fresh and strange again. If we are willing to engage the disorder of much new art on these terms, we find we are less alarmed by its apparent incomprehensibility.

The Excellent Art That No One Sees

ONE OF THE SADDEST aspects of the professional arts in Canada is the waste factor. We are positively profligate with our creative riches. Too much of our created work goes unseen for lack of presentation opportunities. Plays, books, paintings, works of choreography: they surface, often after a prolonged and painful gestation, are briefly visible, then sink into obscurity. Not all of them are wonderful; for some, obscurity is a merciful end. But it is the loss of the good ones that is the tragedy. Anyone who attends the theatre or the concert hall or the gallery with any regularity can think of provocative or interesting works that were seen or heard a few times, then disappeared forever. Who recalls Tom Walmsley's play *Something Red*? ("Explosive, searingly honest dialogue that presents a gripping portrait of the harsh realities of city life," said a reviewer the morning after its 1978 premiere.) Who remembers Winnipeg choreographer Rachel Browne's duet *Interiors,* which Browne herself regards as one of her best works of the 1970s? Sometimes, in the case of a piece of dance or a play, a revival is mounted, and the flame flares for a moment more. But in most cases these works are distant echoes on the wind of reported history. We are confronting the paradox of excellent art that no one sees: a whole lost heritage. How do we deal with this?

Renewed attention to distribution, outreach and public access by our cultural institutions—all of it planned, measurable and accountable—will go far towards solving the painful enigma of invisible excellence. By developing the work(s) of our artists, making our venues for presentation more inviting, and building and reinforcing the notion of collective ownership, we will help ensure the presentation of our threatened heritage. And in preserving that heritage, we will enrich the fabric of the backdrop against which all new art is made, preserving what has gone before as a context for what is to come. More on this a little later.

6

THE ARTS ORGANIZATION

The "big 17" performing-arts organizations make up only 3 per cent of
Canada's 602 non-profit performing-arts groups. They account,
however, for 25 per cent of total attendance, 46 per cent of salaries
and wages, and 41 per cent of operating revenues. (The Stratford Festival
alone accounts for over 8 per cent of all operating revenues.)

—Details extracted from the preliminary analysis
prepared for the Canada Council for the Arts Working
Group on Large Performing Arts Organizations, 2001

HE ORGANIZATIONS THAT deliver arts and culture to the citizens of Canada—our orchestras, theatre and opera companies, dance troupes, publishers, museums and galleries—are an integral part of our country's cultural infrastructure. Some of them have been with us for more than half a century; they have been major contributors to the definition of Canada's culture, they continue to be significant employers of Canadian artists and producers and presenters, and many of them play an important role as pivots of artistic activity and excellence in their home community.

Government funding cutbacks and a general audience decline in the 1990s have hit these organizations hard. The competition for both grants and audiences has become more intense as the range of cultural activities in Canada's towns and cities has broadened; faced with high fixed costs, many organizations have found it hard to manoeuvre. Desperate steps have been taken. At the Toronto Symphony Orchestra, there was both a wage rollback and a raiding of the thought-to-be-sacrosanct endowment fund. At the National Ballet of Canada, the artistic director quit and went to Germany in despair at his financial inability to carry out his vision for the company. The Vancouver Symphony Orchestra, like others across the country, has come perilously close to extinction on more than one occasion. By the end of the twentieth century, the combined deficits being carried by the twenty-nine performing-arts organizations with annual budgets of $3 million or more was $20 million. The Calgary Philharmonic Orchestra was forced into bankruptcy protection. In several cases, the decline has been irreversible; in others, crisis and last-minute rescue has become a recurrent cycle.

Today, Canada's arts organizations of all sizes face challenges and opportunities on a number of fronts. Changing patterns of entertainment choice, together with the changing cultural makeup of Canada, demand a wholesale rethinking of the nature and needs of audiences, as well as new approaches to programming and marketing. At the same time, the looming crisis of management expertise throws a pall of uncertainty over the entire endeavour. And in the area of content and delivery, advances in communications technology will open entirely new avenues of experiment, experience and public access.

There is no question that we need to strengthen the mechanism of professional performance and production at every level. But it is no longer adequate to suggest that the problems will go away when the economy improves or when the government changes. Indeed, some observers go so far as to suggest that the institutions created in the past are no longer adequate to the tasks of today and tomorrow. The challenges that confront today's arts organizations are so profound that they threaten the very foundations of these organizations' existence.

Do we need to reinvent our cultural institutions, to take proper account of the social change we witness all around us? Or can we, by careful adjustment and selective rethinking, reposition and reinforce the existing structure? Perhaps it is in the explorations provoked by these challenges that we will find, finally, the key to making Canada's culture truly and democratically accessible to all Canadians.

Sustainability: Not Just Treading Water

ALARMING NEWS STORIES about the imminent collapse of our most important cultural institutions have been commonplace in recent years, and the cultural community must be situated on a steady economic and operational base if we are to benefit fully from the many ways in which cultural activity can enrich society.

Insistent demands have been heard from the major arts organizations for a commitment from government (the Canada Council for the Arts, primarily) to recognize their importance and their special needs with a guarantee of substantially increased long-term funding. To signal that recognition, they want to see a specific program for large organizations within each discipline, with dedicated funding. Throwing large amounts of money at our major arts organizations would be a solution of sorts, but to have any real impact, far more money would be needed than is currently available. And it would be both unfair and divisive to treat large organizations as a separate division, particularly if that were to divert funds from equally needy areas (the funding of individual artists, for example, without whom the major organizations might just as well be out of business). More useful would be an approach recognizing that the health of the cultural sector depends on the sustainability of the organizations working within it.

Sustainability is a more complicated question than is sometimes assumed. Some critics cry that all would be well if our professional cultural organizations and agencies were run in the same manner as private businesses. This idea has obvious merit, so long as we recognize that an arts organization, as a charitable, non-profit enterprise, is driven by a different agenda from an enterprise in the private sector, and even the largest of them are tiny by commercial standards, so any practices borrowed from the business community must be modified accordingly. Certainly, however, arts organizations and arts funders have increasingly understood that businesslike methods of operation (efficient management, wise governance, realistic goal-setting, careful attention to results, responsiveness to needs of the served community) are essential if we want our cultural organizations to thrive.

In that regard, a support mechanism that has been attracting increasing attention in recent years is a public-cum-private process of support known as arts stabilization, which helps arts organizations help themselves by encouraging them to achieve long-term sustainability within a finite time frame. The idea had its origins in the U.S., when the Ford Foundation began to question whether its funds were being used to optimum effect. Organizations that participate in a stabilization program commit themselves to upgrading their operations, with the aim of achieving a balanced budget and the elimination of an operating deficit. In return, they get professional assessment, advice, assistance and supervision in areas ranging from financial management and strategic planning to market research, audience outreach, fundraising, board development and governance. Providing they meet certain measurements, they also receive, for the duration of the program (usually five years), substantial capital to help them with specific needs, such as the retirement of their accumulated deficits. The capital comes from a central pot to which the public and private participants contribute. When the money is gone, the program ends, ideally leaving a legacy of newly stabilized organizations and a healthier cultural ecology.

What is important here, and indeed in any discussion of require ments imposed by funding agencies on arts organizations, is the organization's right to carry out its artistic mandate as it sees fit. The outcome of the making of art cannot be measured only in terms of tickets sold, seats filled and audiences reached; and any agency that uses the carrot of financial reward as the lure towards strict accountability and sustainable practice runs dangerously close to coercion.

With that caveat in mind, it is nevertheless true that the institutions that emerge successfully from this rigorous process are likely to be better equipped to respond to the challenges presented by the constantly changing cultural field. Crisis management, emergency appeals and repeated "one-time" bailouts, so often defended as obligatory in extreme and life-threatening circumstances, become less likely. These organizations will have been not only stabilized, but stabilized in a sustainable way over the longer term. The entire cultural sector benefits, and its reputation for tiresome theatrics and public hysteria of the wolf-crying kind diminishes.

Although the short-term stabilization support program is essential, it is the long-term effect of these sustainability initiatives that holds the greatest promise. A healthy organization is able to thrive on many fronts. Artistically, it can afford to be far more adventurous in its thinking, responding with spirit and intelligence to the ever-changing opportunities offered within its discipline. Managerially, it is flexible enough to absorb and grow from ever-changing demands in its field, and better able to attract suitable employees. Financially, its upgraded performance gives it a chance to recruit and develop substantial long-term support from the community. An organization that demonstrates this kind of responsibility, accountability and organizational strength—as well as the artistic vision and excellence that are its reason for being—is more likely to win support, from both the private sector and government, than an organization that bases its appeal on artistic strengths alone.

The key to this system's success is its marriage of public money and private. Funding for the stabilization programs (which differ slightly according to needs of various regions) comes on a matching basis from the private purse (foundations and individuals within the client organization's community) and various levels of government. That buy-in at every level is a vital aspect of the program's success.

Early results from the first two cycles of stabilization programs (in Alberta and B.C.) suggested that the system works, giving the groups that participate tools to improve their financial, management and governance structures. Though the programs were initially designed to benefit large and mid-sized organizations, it was found that smaller organizations were in equal need of help with long-term planning, governance, budgeting and management skills. A significant component of the federal government's commitment of new money to the arts, announced in May 2001, was an allocation of $63 million, over three years, to a national strategy for greater sustainability. One-third of that sum was dedicated to assisting the community-based stabilization projects that have been springing up across Canada; the balance was set aside to provide contributions to arts and heritage organizations that do not participate in stabilization schemes, as well as to provide organizations' endowments with funds to match money raised from the private sector.

Offering matching funds is a gesture of faith and support from government that should help organizations increase their donation base. However, it can hardly stop there. While companies accessing this money must demonstrate their commitment and ability to operate in a professional manner, the tune-up factor that is such an essential part of stabilization thinking could be of material benefit as well.

But success with sustainability, like success with so much else in our arts organizations, depends, in the end, on individuals—committed boards and motivated, well-trained, persuasive management.

The Challenge of Management Renewal

A SIGNIFICANT FACTOR in this equation has been the consistent willingness of workers in the arts to provide what amounts to discount labour, or what one arts consultant calls sweat equity. Entire generations of arts professionals have been willing to work for less than the going rate in other professions, presumably out of a belief in the importance of their work, a sense of gratification at being able to make it, and an acceptance of the notion that it is not sufficiently valued by society for them to expect other than meagre recompense. These are the people on whom the non-profit arts structures of this country were largely built. Without their browbeaten devotion, their sense of privilege at being able to do the things they love, our cultural landscape would be far less diverse than it is today.

However, the numbers of these self-sacrificial lambs are dwindling. We are approaching (if we have not already reached) a crisis point in the development of the professional arts in Canada. Individual burnout is endemic in a generation whose careers have been spent in the pioneering, often frustrating task of building our non-profit arts organizations and keeping them on an even business keel. That problem is made more acute by the fact that the succession is far from assured. In the words of a recent report by Tom Lewis and others for the professional associations of Canadian opera, music and theatre management: "The funding cuts of the mid-1990s decimated the ranks of upcoming young managers and now there is a squeeze: the current generation of managers is quitting or retiring and the succeeding generation is insufficient to provide replacements."

We are moving into a period when young management graduates—the best-trained in Canadian history—will have their pick of jobs across the public and private sectors. Why would they opt to become involved in a field with low income prospects and constant economic uncertainty? It is time for a sea change in our approach to the management of our arts and cultural sector.

Veteran arts activist and consultant John Hobday, director of the Canada Council for the Arts, is unequivocal. He believes it is necessary to "build up strategies to attract, recruit, nurture and provide quality professional development opportunities and fair remuneration to the people who are needed on the management side of our arts and heritage organizations. They are the connectors, the people who are absolutely critical in connecting the artists and their activities with their audiences. We need the best and the brightest to do that. Each organization requires a business-skilled, technologically savvy core of really committed people who care passionately about their organization. They need to feel that they are being reasonably treated and fairly remunerated. The working conditions in most of our arts organizations are no longer acceptable."

As government moves towards an era of increased fiscal responsibility and transparency, emphasis will be placed on new approaches to arts management and professionalism. New ways to formulate expected results of arts investment, and new ways to assess those results, will force a more stringent accounting. Many of our large organizations, sniffing the wind, have already put in place effective professional management and governance; the Canada Council for the Arts has itself articulated a results-oriented business plan and detailed codes of governance and ethical behaviour. But much remains to be done in the education and training of the generation of administrators who will be given charge of our arts organizations at this crucial, transformative time.

Pressures to find ways to finance the creation and production of artworks of all kinds—the immediate end product—have diverted attention from the problem of providing effective, efficient and flexible long-term management. But a permanent, workable solution to that problem is fundamental. We must establish a body of individuals with the professional skills to bring that promise to reality and, just as valuable, to be the kind of advocates who can explain to potential funders exactly why the arts are worth funding.

How do we manage this? Many of the details are spelled out by Jocelyn Harvey in her report on an extensive survey of the problem carried out in 2002. Titled *The Creative Management Project,* the study was coordinated by the Canadian Conference of the Arts and the Cultural Human Resources Council. It was funded by the Samuel and Saidye Bronfman Family Foundation (of which John Hobday was executive director until his appointment to the Canada Council for the Arts late in 2002) and the Department of Canadian Heritage. Conducted across the full spectrum of government and non-government agencies, the consultations resulted in a consolidated set of thoughtful and realistic proposals.

Under a set of umbrella guidelines (more targeted research, practical and flexible solutions, more sustained operating funding for arts organizations), the proposals deal with both organizations themselves and the agencies responsible for their funding and operational health. Among the identified priorities for the organizations are the following:

- an increase in the knowledge of and respect for the profession of cultural manager (for instance, by promoting it as a career option in schools, colleges and artists' training institutions, and by creating national awards in the profession)
- the integration of human resources policies and practices into the sector (which would mean, for instance, requiring HR plans to be submitted by arts organizations along with financial and artistic plans when they apply for funds; sharing HR policies and practices

across the sector; and developing succession planning, leadership development and proposals for increasing the involvement of aboriginal and culturally diverse individuals in the field)

- the introduction of pension and benefits packages
- creation of new internship/mentoring programs
- the development of sabbatical-style renewal and reinvigoration opportunities

These are all important suggestions. We know that a proven way for individuals to develop skills and test their creative abilities is through working with people already established in their fields. In the arts, this is a particularly cost-effective way to spread the funding dollar, since it supports the mentor and the apprentice simultaneously. It is a method whose benefits are not limited to creative artists. Targeted mentor, apprenticeship and intern programs would be an effective means of addressing the shortfall in cultural managers and a way to increase aboriginal and minority staff representation in the various cultural industries.

The Canada Council for the Arts has conducted successful mentor/apprenticeship programs in a variety of areas, but the full potential of this simple developmental tool has yet to be exploited. The now-defunct Training Initiatives Program of the Cultural Human Resources Council also provided on-the-job internship and mentoring opportunities with cultural organizations. In Quebec, a scheme has been proposed under which an emerging arts administrator would work alongside a senior manager who is planning to retire or leave the job; the two would split the workload, with the younger taking on more and more of it as the other's departure nears. In a variant of this, the manager of a Vancouver theatre company quoted in the CCA/CHRC study proposed that he act as mentor for a year to a younger administrator, then take a sabbatical, at a reduced salary, while the younger individual ran the company. "I would have the time off to be invigorated and refreshed," he argued. "My company would be in secure and competent hands during my absence; and an emerging leader would have the benefit of on-the-job mentoring and career advancement—it's a win-win-win situation."

Sabbaticals for arts managers is an idea whose time may not yet have arrived, but it looms on the horizon. It can be argued, not entirely soundly, that the senior arts grants awarded to individuals by the Canada Council for the Arts are effectively the arts-field equivalent of academic sabbaticals. They do provide artists with valuable time for the reflection, refreshment and restoration otherwise not available to them; but most of the grants, unlike academic sabbaticals, come with the requirement (or the commitment) of some kind of work as an end product. The evidence we see of creative and managerial burnout suggests that both creators and managers eventually reach a point, just like academics and other professionals, where they need time to recuperate and renew. A humane vision of arts and cultural funding, it could be argued, should include provision of resources to underwrite a serious, properly administered program of sabbatical leave for established professionals throughout the cultural field.

The anecdotal evidence provided in the CCA/CHRC report makes it clear that a substantial investment is needed to upgrade the management of our arts and cultural sector. Ideally, ways should be found to bring business partnerships into play by contributing skill-building techniques and mentoring sessions. Questions of cross-sectoral collaboration, governance and the functions of the boards of non-profit arts organizations have long been neglected; these too must be addressed if there is to be any serious hope of creating a network of stable, healthily functioning cultural organizations ready to face the challenges of making and producing art in the new Canada. It is important for all cultural organizations to actively seek out and recruit individuals who can contribute the specific skills needed at the board level. In the same way, active recruitment of other committed volunteers should be an ongoing activity.

Much of the basic research has already been done. The CCA/CHRC report was augmented by a "proposed action plan for creating winning conditions," prepared by Jocelyn Harvey for the 2003 Chalmers Conference organized by the CCA. This action plan, building on responses to the original report, fleshed out the proposals in specific terms, concentrating on improved human resources policies in the arts and culture sector and recommending a number of direct actions governments and service agencies should take. Rather than waste time and resources redefining the problem, a high-level interdepartmental federal task force should now work with representatives of the principal cultural agencies, advocacy groups and specialist support organizations to finalize an action plan and a timeline. Specifically, what is needed is a comprehensive management development and improvement program that synthesizes the skills, interests and resources of the sectors of government that specialize in management and marketing (not necessarily of the arts).

We should insert here a vital proviso: the costs that will inevitably be incurred in the development of such a program should be covered by new funding, not existing program funds. If, for instance, the program is housed under the umbrella of the Canada Council for the Arts, which would seem logical, additional resources should be provided. Important arguments can be made for such a scheme, but the funds must not be diverted from the support provided for (for example) individual artists, media arts or publishing. Every division of Council support can make a convincing argument for increased funding, and it would be both irresponsible and misguided to short-change any of them.

With that proviso in place, here are some of the necessary management upgrades:

- An improvement in managerial skills overall. (Surveys have shown that a wide variety of management improvement courses and services are available, at a price, in both the public and the private sector. Organizations that fall outside the parameters of stabilization programs should be helped to access these.)
- A focus on improving managerial skills in the cultural field for members of aboriginal communities and under-represented cultural groups. (Internships and mentoring programs are crucial here.)
- Leadership training to help organizations root themselves in their communities. (This creation of a connection between artist and audience is fundamental to survival.)
- Training for arts management professionals in the broader social implications of their work. (This would include training in communication, advocacy and the tools to demonstrate the social relevance and value of their work.)
- Training in board recruitment and renewal techniques. (This would include a new awareness of issues such as governance, accountability and performance evaluation, as well as organizational leadership, long-term strategizing and the ability of board members to plead the cause convincingly.)
- A significant upgrade in working conditions for arts management, covering benefits, pensions, internship/mentoring programs, and sabbatical-style renewal and reinvigoration. Since the provision of benefits like these is beyond the resources of many small arts organizations, a fund should be established on which qualified organizations and individuals could draw.

Even If You Build It, Will They Come?

THE EXPONENTIAL increase in available entertainment is changing the way we entertain ourselves. So much entertainment is on offer, of such variety, that audiences graze the garden of offerings in a daze of anticipation, plucking a blossom here, a blossom there, always moving on to the next best experience—a ticket to the ballet, a hockey game, a movie, the theatre, a gallery, a day of skiing, a round of golf. Increasingly, we prefer to pick and choose our cultural experiences rather than buy them by subscription package. For our arts organizations, matching offerings to ticket buyers is becoming an increasingly precise science, and as the demand grows for a more meticulous accounting for the value of arts subsidy, the temptation to become purely market-driven will intensify.

This issue is complicated by various factors, some of them simple facts of life. What has traditionally been considered as the core audience—baby boomers with no children and some disposable income—is getting older (a factor that directly relates to the dwindling in the ranks of arts management). Ticket prices are rising. The new core audience (and the generation that follows) is going to see the performing arts less frequently than their parents did; Statistics Canada figures show that performing-arts attendance dropped by 5 per cent overall in the 1990s. And young people are leaving our schools and universities with little awareness of or interest in what the professional arts can offer.

Arts groups have tried to combat these trends with a relentless variety of discount deals, catchy program ideas and outreach presentations designed to capture the interest of the schoolchildren who will be the next generation of audiences. If the arts are not part of their lives, what kind of life can the arts expect to have? But the days when theatre and music audiences could be persuaded in large numbers to subscribe to lengthy performance series are over. The subscriber loyalty that brought with it the feeling that you were part of a privileged family is eroding. Discounted prices still sell subscriptions, but in a recent U.S. survey, only 8 per cent of potential classical music customers said they would be "highly inclined" to subscribe. We find our families in other places today, often virtual places where we need no ticket and do not have to dress up. Commitment is hard to develop. Instead, arts marketers find themselves in a constant challenge to attract the casual, single-ticket buyer.

Concert clubs, trial concerts for potential newcomers, singles nights, crossover sales campaigns with other arts groups and shorter, tightly themed subscription packages are all techniques that have been tested. The use of new communications technology holds promise as a low-cost tool for one-on-one subscriber contact presenting special offers, last-minute deals and other initiatives that make the individual feel singled out for attention. Marketers are also learning that what they are selling goes beyond the presentation on the stage or concert platform. User-friendly devices are becoming popular, including large-print programs, sound-amplifying headphones and even—in England's government-subsidized theatres—staff members to walk and feed guide dogs during performances. The National Arts Centre in Ottawa is toying with offering a rebate on the costs of babysitting; in the fall of 2003 the Vancouver Symphony Orchestra became the first orchestra in North America to use large-screen live projections of the conductor and performers in the auditorium.

The point is simple: if you want to bring audiences in, you have to go out and get them. Museums and galleries are no longer the temples to acquisition, prestige and exclusivity that they were in the nineteenth and a large part of the twentieth century. If they are to preserve the position that has always been theirs—guardians of a culture's history, showcase of its created glories, delineators of its present way of life— they must diversify their activities in ways that might earlier have been unimaginable. New approaches to access are needed: electronic access to collections and exhibitions, certainly, but physical access as well. For instance, the high cost of admission to arts and cultural events has always been seen as a hindrance to audience-building. One often-proposed solution to the problem of making museums more accessible is to remove admission charges, thus making the experience more inviting for individuals with limited resources. Interestingly, however, evidence from England suggests that removing admission charges for museums is no guarantee that the number of visits by individuals from lower socio-economic groups will increase. Although visitor numbers increased by up to 111 per cent in the first year of free admission at six London museums, the number of visits they received from the lower three socio-economic groups—which represent half the population—increased only slightly. And the museums complained that their loss of income (only partly compensated for by additional subventions from government, and exacerbated by the additional costs incurred in dealing with larger attendances) was compromising the quality of their presentations and service to the public.

In the theatre, the evidence seems somewhat different. In a 2002 experiment in London aimed at attracting a younger audience, tickets for musical and mainstream theatre were offered at the price of a West End movie ticket. In a city where the cheapest theatre seat is often £20 (about $50), patrons could buy a top-price ticket for the Royal Shakespeare Company, normally selling for £37.50 (around $95), for £11.50 ($29). Early responses to the program were enthusiastic, with thousands of young people taking advantage of the offer, though it was of course too soon to tell whether their enthusiasm was going to turn into a theatre-going habit.

One similarly successful experiment in attracting new audiences in Canada has been the National Arts Centre's Live Rush program. Billed as "the cheapest date in town," the scheme made last-minute NAC tickets available for less than the cost of a movie. A comfortable Live Rush area was created where participants could pick up tickets (bypassing the formal wicket), use computer terminals and socialize. (It was, one participant told NAC director Peter Herrndorf, a great pickup spot.) More than six thousand young people in Ottawa took part in the first two seasons; subsequently, a dozen performing-arts organizations adopted the scheme in Calgary, and the NAC has plans to create similar audience development programs for young single professionals and young married couples, two of the centre's prime target areas. The benefits of Live Rush are obvious: the program helps develop cultural literacy among the young, and it builds the NAC audience. Its principal drawback is equally obvious: the price of tickets is artificially low, even when set against the subsidized cost of production.

Certainly, however, it seems time for the "classical" performing arts to get serious about de-formalizing their methods of presentation. A recent study of music habits in the U.S. and the U.K., published in the Policy Studies Institute's *Cultural Trends* magazine in 2002, showed that the stuffiness of classical music concerts in Britain threatened to turn off an entire generation of potential audiences. Attendance by individuals under the age of forty-seven dropped sharply in the 1990s, and although one in three Britons said they had at some time attended a classical concert, only 12 per cent had done so in the past year. This is not necessarily a measure of lack of interest: close to 40 per cent of eighteen- to twenty-four-year-olds listened to classical music on the radio, though few developed the habit of attending live concerts. Among the reasons cited: the formality, elitism and "authoritarian" image of cultural institutions. Other studies have shown that some would-be audience members are intimidated by what they perceive to be specific requirements of dress or behaviour at arts events.

Ways are certainly being sought to modify and enliven arts presentation. The traditional orchestral concert, for instance, is a fairly standardized affair: people come into a hall, sit in silence facing in a single direction, and listen to a group of individuals, placed in a fairly standardized pattern on a platform, playing instruments. Over the years, various conductors have juggled the traditional onstage fan of players to find a better acoustical balance. Flamboyant producers have from time to time experimented with light or laser shows coordinated with the music being played. Festivals, pops concerts, play readings, groups that combine a social or meet-the-artist element with a ticket, evenings tailored to particular interests—those tactics all seem to be helping to fill the seats. Imaginative programming tied to the historical and contemporary cultural realities of Canada might also enliven the modern audience's interest.

Voice or dance, or both, have sometimes been incorporated into concert presentations. Artistic directors and conductors will often present informal commentaries. Entire musical programs have been built around narrative themes. We must, however, be careful what we wish for, or what we wish on others. Not every artist is comfortable talking to an audience before a performance. For every Bramwell Tovey or Pinchas Zukerman, with their quick wit and practised ease as concert hosts, there is a pianist or a violinist with an acute case of performance anxiety. It is one thing for an individual to put their own emotions and skills at the service of a composer—in effect, to become the tool through which the composer connects with the audience. It is quite another for that same individual to stand before that same audience and speak about the work and the experience. As any actor will tell you, performance is a cloak behind which the individual can hide. Public speaking is, well, speaking in public, and surveys show that in the list of contemporary society's greatest fears we rank it higher than death.

Opera Surtitles are an example of the way arts organizations have been forced to come to terms with changing times, on the level of both technology and audience expectations. Introduced by the Canadian Opera Company in 1983 and adopted by the New York City Opera the following year, the super-inscription of opera dialogue on the proscenium arch originally met serious opposition within the music profession. Some singers refused to perform beneath the projected words. Star mezzo Marilyn Horne, for one, never hid her ambivalence to Surtitles. Director

Peter Sellars told the Los Angeles Times *in 1988 that he would rather leave the lights on and let the audience read. But no longer. Though the debate within the opera community continues to rage (Surtitles have been blamed for bad acting and lazy diction, and praised for the benefits they bring in terms of comprehensibility of plot), the technology has been welcomed by audiences, and Sellars and most other opera directors now use Surtitles as a matter of course. In fact, the practice has spread to the song recital—with Marilyn Horne leading the way. One thing is certain: titling helps demystify opera for newcomers and make it more accessible. And figures from New York and San Francisco suggest it helps develop new audiences as well.*

The new technologies increasingly offer promising tools. Currently in its testing phase is a computer device called the "Concert Companion." Conceived by the former head of the Kansas City Symphony and developed with the help of two Silicon Valley companies and a music professor, the hand-held electronic device provides a running commentary on the music being played onstage, prompting the listener to watch for such subtleties as the reappearance of themes and the varieties of orchestration.

But, given the technological sophistication of the modern theatre, these innovations are surely just beginnings. It must be possible to find ways to marry the crowd-pleasing theatricality of the modern mega-musical with the delicate probings and transcendental splendours of, say, R. Murray Schafer or Alexina Louie without descending to bathos and vulgarity. And what about more crossover between the various art forms? The Center for Contemporary Opera in New York recently offered the opening act of a new opera twice in the same evening—once performed by a team of opera singers, once by a team from musical theatre. What was most interesting of all, however, was the response of the audience. Most wanted to hear a third version that would incorporate the best of both—the beauty of the operatically trained voices, the passion and mobility of the performers from musical theatre.

The entertainment market (which is, like it or not, where our arts producers are located) is a fiercely competitive one. It is not enough for arts organizations to put out their product and expect people to buy it simply because Art is a Good Thing. We live in a world of economic competition; the ballet company and the art gallery are competing for consumer attention with Procter and Gamble and Wal-Mart. These are the big leagues. Customers have a finite amount of time to pay attention to a message, and when they choose to take part in an event they are opting not to take part in a host of others. To encourage them to make that choice, it is vital that arts organizations position their product—the experience they sell—as unique, valuable, rewarding. Given the passion and dedication arts creators and producers bring to their work, one might expect this to be an integral part of their modus operandi; yet all too often, when the financial push comes to shove, one of the first budget items to suffer is marketing and publicity, particularly in low-budget organizations—arguably the ones who are most in need of exposure and can least afford to make that particular economy. Yet profile is primary. Without turning the experience of art into a purely commercial endeavour, there is nothing wrong with encouraging a spirit of entrepreneurism in its marketing and presentation. Sophisticated and audience-friendly techniques can generate the kind of excitement that leads to open access across a wide swath of society.

Canadian arts organizations in our larger centres might think about emulating the experiments of many cities in Europe and the U.S., where museums and galleries operate at visitor-friendly hours and team up to sell single tickets that give access to multiple venues. In Amsterdam, for instance, the city's annual Museum Night in November sells out 25,000 tickets at $22.50—in exchange for which the purchaser gets unlimited access to thirty museums, including transport by bus, boat or tram, from 7:00 p.m. to 2:00 a.m.

Attractive spaces help. Most of our theatres have bars, and some offer snacks. Our museums have restaurants: why not more of our concert halls? Can anything be learned from the movie business, where, to counter the challenge of the VCR, the experience has been enhanced by making viewing spaces more intimate and adding food courts and video-game arcades?

Everything, in other words, is on the table. Nothing is sacrosanct. Coupling respect and intelligence with the free exercise of the imagination, Canada's performing-arts community has the potential to transform the theatrical experience in ways that make it relevant and attractive to new audiences. Developing that interest, stoking the receptivity, is the primary challenge.

The good news about the browsing generation is that it *is* open to the next best experience, in part as a response to the commercialization of youth culture through avenues such as MTV and MuchMusic, and the challenge to the authenticity of rock and pop by star-search shows that create an entirely synthetic form of celebrity. Conditioned by the multimedia hyperstimulus of modern urban life, young audiences are increasingly open to innovative encounters with art. The challenge now is to find ways to engage them without compromising the quality of the artistic product. Young audiences can tell immediately if authenticity is in question, as the Joffrey Ballet discovered when it commissioned *Billboards,* a work to music by Prince. The show was a fleeting success with the young crowd, but it did not translate into new audiences over the long term. In fact, the reverse occurred. Young audiences did not come back, and the traditional ballet audience, who hated the show, stayed away as well. The experiment almost killed the company.

Most organizations are learning that it is important not to intimidate through expectation. Certainly, foreknowledge can enrich the experience, but audiences should be assured they do not have to be experts to enjoy classical music or theatre or dance. You need not be a psychologist to be moved by *The Glass Menagerie,* nor a Freemason to appreciate *The Magic Flute.* The most valuable quality is receptivity, an openness to what the artist has to say and a willingness to make discoveries.

Tools to help audiences on the way to that adventure are helpful. The Canadian Opera Company posts a beginners' guide to opera, Opera 101, on its website. Printed programs are becoming more user-friendly. Pre- and post-performance lobby chats work wonders to heighten audience appreciation and extend the personal pleasure people buy with their ticket, and it would be good to see this approach extended to televised performances. It works, after all, for hockey. Wouldn't it be enlightening to have a mid-broadcast Ballet Coach's Corner, as disputatious as you like, for a televised National Ballet production of James Kudelka's newest sex-and-death allegory? Instant accessibility, instant engagement.

Broader and deeper relationships can be established by arts organizations across disciplines to take advantage of the integrative directions artists are exploring. These relationships could take many forms—cross-disciplinary co-productions, sponsorships, outreach programs, school events. But all would have at their forefront a desire to link the work to the community's interests and issues.

Central to this opening-up of the experience is the need for a shift in mindset on the part of creators, producers and presenters of arts and culture. To borrow terms from economics, this means switching their emphasis from supply to demand. Creators and producers should give fresh attention to the needs of the consumer—invite, in other words, a greater public involvement with art across all segments of the potential audience.

Vancouver Opera is one organization that has taken on the challenge four-square, and the company now makes a habit of working to engage an audience far beyond the traditional opera-house walls. For a production of Carlisle Floyd's *Of Mice and Men,* for instance, it organized forums, seminars, talks and community events in collaboration with mental health, anti-poverty and inner-city agencies. For *Aida,* it staged a controversial panel discussion on the plight of women in wartime, moderated by global issues specialist and former foreign minister Lloyd Axworthy and involving a specialist in ethnic and race relations and a United States human rights worker. For *La Bohème,* it put together a panel of legal and social rights experts to talk about women and poverty. Its community programs include an ambitious education program that involves elementary schoolchildren in writing and presenting their own operas, and a series of talks in the heart of Vancouver's Downtown Eastside before and after each opera. vo general director James W. Wright pointed out that while the community forums "made new friends" for the organization, their more important long-term function was to form new alliances among artists, activists, advocacy groups and community resource centres. Commenting on the vo's Downtown Eastside outreach, Jim Green, at the time the president of the Four Corners Bank, said: "Clichés suggest that opera is screaming and yelling and has nothing to do with ordinary people. Then there are those who think poor people don't deserve to be around art; they need to be around making money. They see poor people as culturally, intellectually and emotionally deprived. Both of these stereotypes are totally incorrect. Opera seems to move Downtown Eastsiders more than anything else I've ever seen. I've seen people come out of their shell in a way I never thought possible. It's transforming them."

Audience-friendly presentation and marketing techniques can help arts companies reach schools, youth groups, members of aboriginal and minority cultures, immigrant societies, the people of the inner cities and the people of rural Canada, whether in person, through storefronts or special events, via the Web or through community connections such as sports organizations and business associations. In every case, imaginative outreach is a key element of successful audience development.

Festivals are particularly useful tools, both for audience development and for presenting new, often risk-taking creations that might not otherwise see the light of day. The biennial Canada Dance Festival, for instance, regularly commissions and co-commissions new work from established and experimental modern-dance companies and choreographers. Often the works are significant additions to the national dance repertory: Holy Body Tattoo's *Circa* and *Perfume de Gardenias* by José Navas, both of which went on to great acclaim across Canada and in Europe, were CDF co-creations in 2000. Festival bookings can also act as leverage for large-scale productions. These factors alone are important reasons for government support of festivals, particularly as arts groups come to terms with the budget-tightening effects of new federal legislation restricting tobacco-company promotion of cultural endeavours.

However, festivals are also an important means of access to live performance for Canadians in all parts of Canada, whether it is something as high-profile as the Montreal Jazz Festival (one of the world's most important) or as modest as a Yukon storytelling festival. Attractively priced, festivals give a diverse audience the chance to connect, within a brief time span, with a wide range of artists and works, particularly in regions where live performance is otherwise in short supply. They are also a convenient, cost-effective way to introduce Canadian audiences to foreign artists, giving them a chance to see how the local talent measures up on the international scene. Festival audiences seem more willing to accept experimentation in what is often an informal setting. Not least, festivals bring a sense of celebration to a community, and they can often generate significant sponsorship from the private sector.

Other approaches? A 2001 report on marketing and audience development by small new-music organizations in Canada made the point that many contemporary arts groups are like the disappearing small retailer—modest sales volume, limited public reach, dramatically high costs in relation to sales. "In truth," wrote the report's authors, Lendre Kearns and Judy Harquail, "what we would really like to recommend is that someone do for new music what 'Particip-Action' did for physical fitness." They added the rueful caveat: "Of course, it's a dream, and unlikely ever to become reality."

In fact, there is no reason why someone (logically, the federal government's Department of Canadian Heritage, with its lengthy experience in organizing national campaigns) should not take up this challenge. A "ParticipAction" campaign for the arts, carefully pitched and intelligently structured, could do as much to stretch the country's cultural muscle as Health Canada's much-emulated physical fitness promotion campaign did to transform the lifestyle of Canadian couch potatoes.

Ultimately, though, creators and producers must trust the inclination, taste and wisdom of their intended audience. Popularize as they might, survey as they might, not everything is for everyone, and no arts and culture organization can be all things to all people. Accessibility is not the same thing as universality. Some organizations will become expert in a particular musical or theatrical or choreographic style; some will concentrate on experimentation and research in their particular field; some will focus their energies on youth or cultural minorities. Making something available to everyone does not mean everyone is going to take up your offer, nor should they be expected to. In the end, we are confronted (or comforted) by a matter of trust: trust in the artist, trust in the audience and trust in the ability of them both to find each other.

The Democracy of Accessibility

THE COMING TOGETHER of old and new cultures is one of the great definers of Canada in the first part of this century. How our artists and arts groups embrace the potential of that pluralism, both in terms of the art they make and in terms of the audiences they seek, will play a large part in determining their robustness and continuing relevance.

In the new cultural climate of Canada, a new openness is called for. Of course, the purity of the act of artistic creation must never be compromised, and we must be alert to the dangers of trying to force round pegs into square holes: the value of the experience of some traditional forms of artistic expression lies precisely in their embodiment of those traditions, and there are limits to the degree to which these art forms can be made more broadly accessible without compromising their integrity. But greater efforts must be made to give marginalized groups means of entry. And the diversity of our cultures must find stronger expression. If we wish to lay valid claim to democracy, and to achieve our goal of Canadians working together to shape a collective identity and a collective future, the disparate peoples who make up the new Canada must be heard, heeded and helped.

It is no accident that the crisis years of many of our most important arts producers are coinciding with these major population changes. These organizations can no longer rely on replicating the artistic and box-office successes of the past. If they are not to be cast up gasping in the shallow backwaters, they must find new and bold ways to return to the mainstream, to reintegrate themselves with a society that is in danger of becoming indifferent to their existence. A recognition of this new reality will be integral to the success of all Canada's cultural institutions and agencies. It is not simply a matter of adapting current practice and assimilating new clients; it is a matter of fundamentally reorienting.

Newcomers to Canada, all the people of our diverse cultures and their children must have the opportunity to contribute to the cultural mix of the society in which they live and to which they pay their taxes. This will happen only if the broad cultural community recognizes the duality of its obligations: to make its products accessible to the widest possible audience and to embrace the involvement of all Canadians in its activities. It can even be argued that it is the duty of those who are privileged to work in these areas (and who do so with the assistance of the public purse) to ensure that the widest possible range of expression is placed before the widest possible spectrum of interested audiences.

Before any of this can happen, an arts organization needs to recognize why its audience should want to be there. This seems like a simple truism, but the pressures of ensuring that tickets are sold can sometimes overwhelm the reason for presenting a performance in the first place. A performance is a collaboration and communion between performers and those performed to, achieving what both hope will be a transcendence—certainly, at least, an experience that is in some way provoking or pleasurable and a means to insight and joy.

New audiences may approach traditional forms with very different expectations. And dialogue will be useful only if the basis of difference is understood. Play a piece of Persian music on a Western piano and all you get is apparent dissonance. Exchange is necessary. That means new ways to engage existing audiences and new ways to reach new audiences, particularly in Canada's aboriginal and minority cultures. It means more user-friendly programs, aimed at reaching a variety of communities, building new audiences and extending the organization's reach. It also means long-term work to enlist members of these diverse communities not merely as members of the audience but as staff people, board members, grant-getters, donors and sponsors.

This should not be understood as another tiresome argument for political correctness. The ideal outcome would be the kind of art-making that takes no consideration of ethnic background in its audiences. Cross-cultural creativity is already the source of some of the most intriguing and provocative works in Canada's experimental music and dance communities. (Look at Vancouver's Kokoro Dance, with its blend of Western contemporary dance, modern jazz and Japan's post-Hiroshima butoh; Montreal choreographer Roger Sinha, cross-fusing influences from his native India and his adopted West; or Vancouver's Mandala Arts and Cultural Centre and Vancouver Moving Theatre, bringing together performers from many cultures to present a multidisciplinary collaboration based on the classic Asian epic, the *Ramayana*.) Some of the most exciting contemporary Canadian literature makes migrancy and cultural interchange both background and main theme.

While it takes time for influences to filter out to the broader community, and while we must be wary of the dangers of misappropriation (though not excessively so), there is no reason why the cultural traditions of Canada's indigenous and immigrant peoples could not inspire new works for mainstream cultural providers. A willingness to embrace experiment, to see change as potential rather than threat, and to recognize cultural fusion (as well as cultural difference) as an element of our shared future is integral to the thinking that will separate the survivors from the doomed.

Dramatic art must address all the people. By this, I do not just refer to the working class, but all social levels at once: scholars and craftsmen, poets and shopkeepers, those who govern and those who are governed, in short, the vast human family in which we find both the powerful and the unassertive. I think that the theatre's most important mission is to bring together the members of this large audience with the same ideas and feelings. Dramatic art must address them all, convince them all, and guide their common efforts.

— FIRMIN GÉMIER, actor, director and founder of Théâtre National Ambulant, a travelling theatre of thirty-seven wagons pulled by eight steam tractors active in France in the early twentieth century

Measuring Success

HOW DO WE MEASURE the success of attempts to broaden audiences? In Holland, the government has established a numerical formula that allows it to calculate the success of arts groups in improving their delivery. Alongside a complex and flexible set of other criteria, performing-arts groups are expected to generate 15 per cent of their annual income from the box office, to set aside 3 per cent of their grant income for developing new audiences (particularly youth and cultural minorities), and to meet a certain target in terms of subsidy-per-ticket-sold ratio. All these factors are taken into consideration by granting bodies, though care is taken to situate them in the specific context of each applicant.

It is tempting to suggest that direct assessment of an organization's impact on its chosen community should be built into the process by which decisions about grants are made. Not only would this approach go far towards disarming critics who complain about public spending on the arts, it would also provoke the organization into rethinking its relationship to the community. How does an arts organization expose youth to its work, for instance? What efforts does it make to reach out to the broader community? What role does it play in involving diverse cultures in its activities?

These are all definable, measurable objectives, and those who protest that they have nothing to do with the making of art are missing the point. If society is to underwrite the activity of cultural organizations, it should legitimately expect some kind of delivery on the investment. Ultimately, we all benefit. To impose this kind of accountability on our professional arts and heritage community, its advocates argue, simply requires them to do what they should be doing in the first place: figuring out ways to stay connected to their audience. Most of all, this approach prepares the ground for genuine integration of professional creative activity into the mainstream of society.

What this notion can lead to, however, is the demand that arts organizations justify themselves principally in financial terms. And we must beware of becoming overzealous in applying that argument. Results-based management may be a popular mantra in business, and there is no question that some of our arts organizations could be oper-ated more efficiently. But we must not fall into the trap of allowing these demands to stifle the experiment and unexpectedness that are at the heart of creative activity.

Already, one problem (some would say one intended effect) of government parsimony in arts funding is the way it discourages risk-taking by producers and performers. When your vessel is in danger of sinking, your first priority is to keep it afloat. Factor in a shrinking audience and escalating production costs, and the almost irresistible inclination is to play it safe, retrench, consolidate.

But art, as cannot be repeated too often, is a matter of speculation and imagination, hope and inspiration, bold experiment and noble failure. With the greatest will in the world, the demand for account-ability can be pushed only so far. A point of understanding and com-promise must be reached between those who hold the purse strings and those who do the dance. For that to happen, it is time for arts organizations to renegotiate their significance to society.

Renegotiating Significance

THE IDEA OF GIVING the arts back to the people requires that arts organizations take careful stock of what they are doing when they set out to expand their audiences. Currently, arguments for the democra-tization of the arts and culture usually involve getting more people through the doors and into the seats for activities that already exist— finding ways to sell more tickets to the same types of events.

If this approach has worked, it has worked only to a small degree. For all the well-meant attempts to diversify the market, the symphony/opera/ballet/museum audience is still widely regarded as a coterie of the initiated and the privileged, and its makeup (in terms of social, economic and educational factors) varies little from decade to decade. The reason, it could be argued, is that the sector's sought-after audience is one that already shares the sector's interests. That becomes what has been called a self-reinforcing system of exclusion.

The greatest challenge that arts organizations face is the need to define a new role for themselves. As the attitudes of society change, so do society's demands on its arts and culture providers. If they expect (and accept) substantial public money in support of their activities, they must re-evaluate their role as mediators of our cultural identity. They must redefine themselves and their function in relation to the community they serve, then use that definition as a measuring stick of their success as a public entity.

The questions to be asked are fundamental. What does an organization do? Who is it serving? What is its role in the community? Is it valid, for instance, for a publicly funded theatre company to cater to the tastes, values and interests of a specific sector of the community—even a majority sector—at the expense of the tastes and interests of that community's minorities? If that *is* a valid course to follow, how can an organization expect (or find ways) to be valued and esteemed by the populace at large? Alternatively, might there be innovative ways in which the tastes and interests of the community's minorities can become part of the organization's mandate and activities?

These are not easy questions. They strike to the heart of democracy under the pressure of modern demographics. They throw into relief some long-held assumptions about what arts organizations do. When theatre companies or ballet troupes or galleries choose works to perform or artifacts to display, those choices inevitably involve the rejection of other possibilities. Is it unavoidable that they advance certain visions and values at the expense of others? Might core values become diluted by an inrush of contending views? Is that necessarily a problem? Where and how does the arts organization of the twenty-first century accommodate the intercultural jostle of the community that surrounds it, the community it serves?

The debate is likely to be a hot one. Inevitably, discord will arise. But assiduously pursued and honestly answered, these are questions that will provide our arts organizations with a more penetrating rationale for audience growth than the mere need to sell more tickets and, in the case of orchestras, to use more of the services they are contracted to buy from their musicians. The answers might provide arts and cultural organizations with an entirely new way to position themselves in relation to their community—and thus to demonstrate their relevance and worth. It is a matter of renegotiating significance.

That significance will be dictated to a large degree by the evolving forms and functions of society. One important element of this changing definition of the way we live together has been touched on earlier: society's growing demand for individuals who can make moral and ethical choices informed by a mature vision of cultural priorities. This involves being able to think for the long term; it also involves being open to the intuitive, non-rational solution. Creative activity educates us for uncertainty, and cultural organizations are likely to find much of their relevance to audiences in the coming decades is rooted in their ability to stimulate ethical debate through imaginative expression.

Our vision of what we mean by community and city liveability is undergoing radical reassessment. In an era when the individual act is both threatened and encouraged by technological forces, creative opportunity, cultural diversity and an openness to eccentricity all help, as we have already seen, to develop a civic climate in which the individual spirit and imagination can flourish.

Given these developments, it seems clear that the relevance of arts and cultural organizations will need to be rooted in far more than the mere provision of connection to cultural experience. In particular, as scientific advances bring questions of morality and ethics to the forefront of social discourse, arts organizations will have to recast, in far more accessible terms, their traditional role as agents of moral and ethical reflection.

It is time for the modern arts organization to play a more active role in giving voice to the multiplicity of cultures that make up modern Canadian society. At the heart of the notion of free cultural expression lie the humanistic values that our society has agreed are of lasting importance—democracy, respect for the other, individual freedoms, respect for life, open debate, and the expression of conflicting or variant views. Galleries and museums, in particular, have immense potential as testing grounds for new visions of how we live together, new ways to establish shared values. Our theatres can be meeting places where Canadians from all backgrounds share their stories in an ongoing dialogue.

This is not an argument in favour of using the arts and culture sector as a tool for social engineering, though it may sound suspiciously like it. But as the role and makeup of the modern city evolve, the opportunity exists for the cultural sector to establish (perhaps more accurately, reclaim) for itself a role that places it firmly at the centre of public debate and cultural growth. By encompassing the voices and dreams of the diverse cultures that make up modern Canada, the cultural sector can play a significant role in the evolution of Canadian society.

In redefining this complex role of moral/spiritual/social mediation, arts organizations will have to forge new partnerships across society—partnerships that signal their readiness to descend from the heights of Olympus and be part of the daily world, and their willingness to become facilitators of creative experiment and intercultural dialogue at the grassroots level. Their partners will come not only from government, but from the entertainment industry, the technology sector and other areas of private enterprise, since it is here that the broadest immediate contact can be made with modern society.

At its simplest, it is a matter of creating a new climate for imaginative play—environments where individuals of all ages, backgrounds and walks of life can explore creative possibilities in an unhurried, unthreatened setting. It is about fostering the spirit of innovation, about encouraging new ways of thinking. About devising fresh approaches to difficult dilemmas.

The advances of technology make new partnerships between the cultural sector and other areas of society both easier to forge and easier for the dubious to accept. Innovative variations on the model of the theme park, for instance, might offer a mix of interactive cultural and technological experiences, holographic performance and Web access integrated with a state-of-the-art science centre and a digitalized natural history museum.

In Singapore plans are afoot to revamp the popular Sentosa Island entertainment resort complex through a series of attractions that fuse art, business and technology.

Public libraries have the opportunity to become pivots for community cultural activity. England's Learning Place Consortium, for example, has come up with what it calls a "democracy buildings" proposal, under which civic buildings are remodelled to improve access to lifelong learning and public services. The library would be the anchor in a centre that integrated such civic services as information, health and lifestyle, and adult education. We hardly need to stop there. The public library, rethought and redefined, could become a true centre for cultures, a free space celebrating the colours, tongues and stories of the country's peoples. The public library, in this vision, would become a twenty-first-century agora: meeting place, marketplace, centre of debate and cultural exchange. Housed in the building might be public and private collections of art and objects that link us as a community to our pasts and point us to our future. Strategically located throughout the complex would be spaces offering an ongoing program of readings, talks, forums, demonstrations and performances that draw not only on academic resources but on the full cultural spectrum of the city. Some of the spaces would be large, some small and intimate. Some could feature state-of-the-art digital delivery, high-tech sites equipped to handle (perhaps some years ahead, but coming) 3-D, real-time, Web-based theatrical presentation. Individual booths throughout the site could provide Web access to the online art collections of the world's great museums. Shops, commercial galleries and restaurants around the plaza and on nearby streets would reinforce the multicultural theme and encourage cross-cultural exchange.

Economic and scientific modernization succeeds when it is accompanied by cultural creativity that revolutionizes the way we see the world.
—CHARLES LEADBEATER, *Living on Thin Air: The New Economy*

As I have argued, a widespread recognition of the lasting value of imaginative play will be key to the development of more involved, thoughtful and responsible citizens. This means that in all these schemes, interactivity would be central. Modern society has allowed much of our experience of the arts and culture to slip into a negotiated deal based on spectatorship: we buy a ticket, and that purchase gives us the right to witness an act of art. This is valuable to the extent that witnessing the act can lead an individual to new ways of thinking, new ways of perceiving the world. But today's cultural institutions must also embrace the idea of individual creative action. The rethought library, for instance, might serve as the access point for public involvement with the online creative network proposed later in this book. The educational wing of a symphony orchestra or a theatre company might include collaborative creations with schools—not necessarily for public performance, but as hands-on demonstrations of the ways creative activity can kick-start the imagination.

However, even as we nudge our cultural community towards these exciting and uncharted territories, it is as well to issue a caveat or two.

It is crucial that new partnerships, particularly with the private entertainment sector, do not turn into exercises in empty populism. Market-driven entertainment identifies and co-opts the creative edge for its own purely economic purposes. Popular culture has a habit of sucking the marrow of anarchy from the bones of young revolutionaries in the fields of music, design, fashion and media arts—even in the streets—and serving it up in homogenized bites.

We must also be wary of the seductions of the digital age. We talk of the democratizing powers of the Internet, but it is important to ensure that the interactivity the Net provides is not merely a one-way exchange. Pressing a button to elicit a particular response in a computer game may seem like a free decision, but the options provided have been preselected by the programmer, and all of the outcomes are predetermined. Despite the impression that we are making independent choices, we merely follow, from button to button and link to link. Allowing someone else to think for us is what the entertainment industry desperately wants us to do; it aims to make us docile and manipulable as consumers, all the while deluding us into thinking that we are in control of our choices. The development of creativity and ingenuity—the necessary tools of the information economy—requires hands-on involvement and true open-endedness.

This redefinition of the role of cultural agencies will also depend on the vision and commitment of our cities and municipalities. Civic involvement with culture has until recently tended to be measured in infrastructure (a new concert house, a refurbished theatre) and arts grants. Community arts events are becoming increasingly popular, and the concept of art in education is slowly catching on. It is easy enough to identify the traditional players—orchestra, opera, art gallery, ballet company, museum. Harder to grasp is the way culture permeates the community in a rich, constantly shifting complexity—community centres, libraries, festivals, reading clubs, choirs, private galleries, experimental dance co ops. The attitude that the arts and culture are specialist tastes persists.

This process of change could become much faster and more effective if consideration of culture became an integral, mandated element of planning throughout government. Our cultural leaders could work with politicians and civic leaders to find new ways both to integrate cultural issues into the mainstream of social debate and to facilitate public involvement with creative activity. At the local level, that would mean the automatic inclusion of cultural arguments in the decision-making process covering everything from the city budget to transportation, from education to urban development. This would sharpen awareness of the economic and social values of cultural activity at the neighbourhood level and also increase the likelihood of its application in innovative, exploratory ways. Central to this is a deepened political commitment to the centrality of cultural activity in our lives. Culture's broad social benefits—measured as an improved sense of social inclusion, for instance—should form a solid plank in any platform for civic policy and planning.

7

THE SHOCK OF THE
NEW TECHNOLOGIES

With an incisive irony and a joyful subversiveness, General Idea play-
fully and intelligently appropriated the language and the aesthetics of
the mass media. With its unique creative approach, General Idea
mastered the art of critically dissecting media methods. Their role as
video practitioners, contemporary arts pioneers, curators, publishers, and
general avant-garde bon vivants set a precedent that present-day arts
collectives and artists continue to emulate. Rarely has a group of artists
produced such a coherent yet diverse body of work, one that has
created shock waves that continue to resonate.

— Citation at the presentation of the 2001
Bell Canada Award in Video Art to Toronto's
General Idea collective

MAX DEAN IS one of Canada's leading artists in the area where art and science intersects. In the early 1990s, he spent three years working on his kinetic sculpture, *As Yet Untitled,* a robotic creature programmed to select individual photographs from a collection of discarded family photos and carry them to a shredder. The creature performs this action relentlessly. However, if an audience member activates a pair of hand-shaped sensors connected to the machine, the robot deposits the photographs not in the shredder but in a bin for archiving. The audience member is thus directly implicated in the destruction or preservation of a fragment of human history. "Even doing nothing is a decision," said Dean when the work was first displayed. "Whatever one does is a public act."

Dean's exhibit *The Table* has been created over a number of years in increasingly sophisticated versions in collaboration with U.S. control systems scientist Raffaello d'Andrea. A fully autonomous robotic table installed in a room in a museum selects a viewer and attempts to establish a relationship with that person. "They soon become absorbed in their interaction with the table, anticipating what it might do and how to respond to its advances," Dean has explained. "Why has or hasn't it moved? Why is one person picked and not another? If a selected viewer wishes, a conversation with this table is possible. While the table discovers the body language of the visitor, that person, in turn, can learn to interpret the table's behaviour and have an engaging relationship with this machine, while others watch." Throughout the encounter, the table monitors the visitor's reactions and modifies its behaviour accordingly, and it remains "loyal," making every attempt to stay with the person it has chosen. It is, however, an object in a museum; when the visitor departs, the table must stay, trapped in a room with a doorway too narrow for exit.

Be Me is an installation in which the viewer sits in a chair facing a microphone, beyond which is a screen bearing an image of the artist's face. Using techniques of digital animation and military surveillance, Dean worked with technicians to evolve a system whereby the facial gestures and the spoken words of the viewer are replicated by the image on the screen. It is a disturbing experience, raising questions of who is manipulating whom and whose portrait is being displayed.

The New Technologies and Creativity

THE INTERMARRIAGE OF science and art is not a new notion. It was commonplace in the time of the Renaissance, and it has been endorsed in more recent times by great minds, among them the nineteenth-century German philosopher-sociologist Georg Simmel, who shared the Renaissance view of art, science and religion as holistically integrated; German physicist Max Planck, who believed that the scientist must use an artistic imagination; and the English scientist-philosopher Jacob Bronowski, who drew parallels between the creation of works of art and the discoveries of science.

The introduction of an oil-based medium to the art of painting in the fifteenth century was an early marriage of science and art. The invention of photography in 1939 was another. Picasso's explorations of geometry, photography and cinematography led him to new visions of how to represent the human eye's perception of space; *Les Demoiselles d'Avignon* was his first great breakthrough. Today's artists are embracing the possibilities—still in their infancy—of the new digital technologies.

Some scientists argue that trying to merge art and science trivializes both. London embryologist and science writer Lewis Wolpert, for instance, argues that science, unlike the arts, is "a collective endeavour in which the individual is ultimately irrelevant—geniuses merely speed up discovery ... How different are all the arts. No Shakespeare—no *Hamlet*; no Picasso—no *Guernica*." Moreover, he suggests, a work of art is capable of many interpretations and has moral content, whereas there exists only one correct scientific explanation for any set of observations, and scientific knowledge has no moral or ethical content.

We should also be aware of the potential dangers of this intermarriage. Modern neuroscience, it has been pointed out, has the potential to destabilize such notions as spirituality and intuition—notions at the heart of art-making—by describing rationally the unmagical mental processes and chemical reactions by which these phenomena occur. If humanity comes to the conclusion that there is nothing beyond what is seen—that life is finite, that there is no enduring human "soul," that biochemistry and neuroscience have an explanation for everything—what might this do to the creative spirit, the quest to express that which is beyond the tangible? Certainly we must not succumb to the madness that invests the new technology with the answers to the future. As Goethe warned in *Faust,* technology will not be our salvation. The new technology—be it a pencil or a computer, a video camera or a paintbrush—is simply a tool for the expression of the artist's vision.

The dream of total creative unity among the disciplines—Wagner's *Gesamtkunstwerk* or "total art"—is inextricably tied to our dreams of a unified, coherent vision of existence: the perfectibility of humanity, achieved through artistic expression. It is not likely to happen, not even with the aid of the new magic of digitization. In the age of the individual, we attach too much importance to our creative diversity. However, what *is* possible—what has begun to happen—is the emergence of a new manner of making art. This new art form will be one that draws on the new technologies (and modifies itself as they themselves are modified) to offer artists an additional way in which they can express themselves. Clearly, it is futile and ultimately defeating to draw lines of separation, as the Romantics liked to do, between the arts and the sciences. One informs the other. As Einstein reminded us in the first pages of this book, they are united by our gravitation to the mysterious.

History shows that the sciences and technology have never flourished in the absence of a similar flourishing in the arts.
    —ROBERT ROOT-BERNSTEIN, *The Chronicle of Higher Education*

Cities in Civilization author Peter Hall, like many others, argues that the principal driver of the society of the twenty-first century will be information technology, because it will make possible so many changes and improvements in the way society operates. But the "killer applications" of the new technology, the acts of the imagination that will actually work these transformations, will come, he believes, from a cross-breeding of artists and scientists. Hall calls them "techno-bohos"—a new breed of high-tech bohemians bridging the divide between the arts and the sciences, particularly the computer sciences.

This cross-fertilization is already happening. Until recently, we expected art forms to react to innovation from within their own long-established formal traditions, traditions that originated some-times centuries ago. Serious Western music, for instance, has been modified by diverse influences—African, Japanese, Indonesian, cen-tral European—but it has always absorbed those influences into its own overall structure.

Today, however, innovation has emerged in radically modified art forms: digital art, video art, Web art. In Canada, it was a cross-fusion of experimentation by National Research Council scientists and the National Film Board that led to the beginnings of computer animation technology in Canada four decades ago. But the interaction of art and science is a notion that has caught the attention of the time, not least because of the astonishing advances that are being made, virtually on a daily basis, in the communications technologies. The collaboration of Canadian artists Janet Cardiff and George Bures Miller in their audio-video installation piece *The Paradise Institute,* which won an award at the 2001 Venice Biennale, is a high-profile case in point.

It has been argued that what we are seeing is effectively a new Renaissance. Artists are discovering a source of technological sophis-tication that, until now, has been untapped outside the scientific research community. In the process, artists and scientists are discover-ing that the famous two cultures of C. P. Snow were nothing more than the elements of a myth created to explain a simple unwillingness on the part of two specialist groups to comprehend the value of what the other did. Today, they work together, reuniting the pragmatism of science with the mystical and the unprovable in new forms of artistic expression. Both groups, as Harvard's Rhonda Shearer and Stephen

Gould have pointed out, are exploring the same topics: human life, the universe, eternity and what might lie beyond. Both appreciate elegance, structure and clarity. And both make their best discoveries in the same way: through intuition, luck and creative inspiration. Robert Hughes, in *Culture of Complaint:The Fraying of America,* suggests that the technological potential is so great that a new type of art will emerge, equally devoted to substance and to form: the medium, in other words, will be at least part of the message.

In Britain, where "sciart" has been funded seriously since 1997 (the same year that *Nature* magazine began to run a weekly section on interactions between art and science), projects have ranged from a scheme in which mathematicians and jugglers collaborated to create better juggling acts to one in which archeologists and historians worked with musicians to reconstruct ancient instruments and deduce how they might have been played.

Max Dean's experiments in using robotics to make artistic statements are only one example of what is happening in the vanguard of artistic creativity in Canada. The experiments of Thecla Shiphorst and her colleagues at Simon Fraser University in developing interactive computerized choreography programs have attracted international interest. In Montreal, the Society for Arts and Technology (SAT) has since 1996 facilitated collaborations among artists and scientists in the area of digital technology, staging public performances as well as providing multi-purpose studio spaces for video art and electronic music experiment.

Meanwhile, the Canada Council for the Arts is working with the National Research Council on a pilot program to place artists in science laboratories. Launched in 2003, the program places two practising artists in research establishments with the intent of discovering how far cross-fertilization can push creativity. Catherine Richards, from Ottawa, won one of the two-year, $75,000 fellowships; the other went to Vancouver's Alan Storey.

Storey has a long history of incorporating engineering principles into his work. Among the public sculptures he has made are a giant pendulum in a bank atrium; a wooden walkway on which each step causes steam to be forced through a series of overhead barrels, creating calliope-like musical sounds; and a structure of five elevator-like blocks that rise and fall in exact replication of the activity of the elevators inside a nearby building, while the footprints of those using the elevators, picked up by sensors beneath the carpeting, are projected on a screen—"so," as he explains, "from a standing position on the plaza, an observer would be able to look up and see the movement and use of the inner workings of the building represented in a formal yet abstracted public realm." Under the CCA-NRC program, Storey is working with a Vancouver laboratory on ways to incorporate the vocabulary of fuel cell technology into his artwork.

Richards has been deeply involved with scientific experiment for over a decade and has won various awards for her work incorporating aspects of the new technologies in media arts. One of her best-known pieces, *Charged Hearts,* commissioned by the National Gallery of Canada, features glass hearts under bell jars—lift the jar and a magnetic field causes a cloud of gas to glow and pulsate like a human heart. She will spend her research time working with scientists on aspects of virtual technology and visual media such as the medical devices that allow scientists to view images inside the human body.

A number of ground-breaking conferences on creativity in the arts and sciences have already been held. Much more facilitation of research and exploration in these areas is needed, not only from the Canada Council, with its inevitable emphasis on the arts, but from other granting bodies in government, from industry and from the universities.

I would definitely say this is the dawning of a new Renaissance. We've been through this great era of specialization, but the Internet is now

*linking so many of those different areas of interest that there's a great
need for integrating ... We don't know the benefits of this approach yet.
But one thing's for sure. We can't just sit in our labs and not get involved.*
— PETER HACKETT, vice-president, National Research Council

What the future holds is impossible to say. Inevitably, this new
form of art will be profoundly influenced by the eclectic cultural
makeup of modern Canada. Perhaps what will emerge is a form of
art-making that combines this new democracy of creative possibility
with a new democracy of access to Canada's multiple cultural influences. Who knows what it might look and sound like? We are only
beginning to tap into the potential of this interplay, and that potential
can only become greater as the technologies grow more sophisticated and our artists become more comfortable with these remarkable new tools. What we do know is that the new technologies—
advances in digitization, miniaturization, and the new information
and communications technologies, for instance—present the cul
tural community with the potential to reach a far more diverse audience for the arts and culture than it has ever known.

The New Technologies and Distribution

YOU COME HOME from work at the end of a tiring day and press the
button that activates your personal performance centre. A screen parts
to reveal a wall-sized display monitor offering a three-dimensional,
full-sized performance of *The Rez Sisters* at Manitoba Theatre Centre or
a recital by Ben Heppner at the new Toronto opera house or a poetry
slam at Vancouver's Western Front. It's not two-dimensional television, with its pokey little figures and its less-than-lifelike sound. It's
not even the movie house, though you are free to scatter popcorn on
the floor if you want extra atmosphere. To all intents and purposes, it's
the performance experience that you once had to go to the theatre to

find, minus the person with big hair in front of you and the wrapper cracklers behind.

Or maybe you are out for the day on your sailboat, or in the mountains, or in a city park. You feel the urge to watch Evelyn Hart and Rex Harrington dance *Onegin* or listen to a reading of Floyd Favel's play-in-progress or do a virtual tour of Janet Cardiff's latest installation, so you tune in your on-wrist flexiport, snap out the folding LCD screen and presto, there it is, yours.

This may sound speculative, but in some form or other, this is our future. It is a dozen years away at most. Few of us are prepared for it, yet the phenomenal progress in information and communications technologies will permanently transform the way we absorb our cultural experience, the way we "consume" culture and the arts. Just as innovative forms of creation will transform how cultural products are made, new, probably startling, even unwelcome paradigms of distribution and access must be considered. No cultural organization will be able to ignore the increasing demand for universal access to information—a term that includes creative "product." Performance delivery is being revolutionized, and the challenge offers a rare opportunity for radical rethinking of the way we experience performance. It is a tidal wave of change that threatens to submerge any organization unwilling to adapt.

One promise of the headlong digital advance is technology that will allow anyone with access to the necessary equipment to experience virtual renditions of original artworks—without leaving home. The implications of such access are profound. Why bother to fight the crowds to see the great Rembrandts of the Hermitage, or the Impressionists in the Musée d'Orsay, or the Carrs and Riopelles in the National Gallery of Canada, when we can conjure from the ether, in the comfort of our own dens, an exact, three-dimensional replica of a painting, and eventually a sculpture or other installation, so meticulously rendered that it is impossible to distinguish from the original? If we follow the ripples of this argument out, what will this availability do to our valuation of this work, tied as that is at present to rarity and authenticity? Will the new technologies lead us to a saner relationship with art, away from our obsession with monetary value and back towards a concern with what the artist is trying to express? Our answers to these questions will tell us much about how we as a society truly value art and art-making.

The experts may wrestle with the dilemma of an object and its uniqueness, but a vast new audience will nevertheless exist for the delivered experience. A gallery's physical location will still matter to those who want (and are able) to visit the primary artwork. But electronic access to the gallery's holdings at the interested individual's convenience—with all the supplementary materials and interpretive tools that technology allows—will assume a central significance. Apply the same convenience of access to high-quality performance, and we begin to get the measure of how radically the new technology will transform our lives.

This all holds great promise for Canada. Already, the country's extensive communications networks place Canadians among the most connected people in the world. The new digital technologies could finally provide the means to vanquish the vastness of Canada's geography, a challenge that has always thwarted the dream of nationwide access to the products of our arts and culture sector. Despite the indefatigable efforts of arts-touring networks such as Debut Atlantic, Jeunesses Musicales and Overture Concerts, which have for many years brought the experience of the live performing arts to remote regions of Canada, many Canadians have never had access to anything but a sampling of the great resources of our museums, our galleries and our performing artists.

What does all this mean to an organization like the Stratford Festival, the National Ballet, the Orchestre symphonique de Montréal? Or organizations like One Yellow Rabbit, La La La Human Steps or the

Vancouver Chamber Choir? What does it mean in terms of ownership of performance? How does it change the notion of box office? Of touring? Of live performance versus recorded? What will it mean in terms of security or duration of employment? How will performing-arts groups compete against (or integrate with) the proliferating electronic entertainment media? Is some form of production concentration a likelihood?

What does it mean for the notion of a dedicated cultural space—the theatre, the concert hall, the opera house, the museum?

It is unlikely that we will ever abandon the live experience of dance or music or theatre, with its immediacy, its unpredictability and its unrepeatability. However sophisticated the means of delivery become, there will always be a need for the communal experience of art, for the church-going effect of sharing a transformative experience with others. And to judge from the building boom that is going on, no one in the business of culture seems likely to give up soon on the live visitor or on contemporary methods of attracting the visitor's interest. (In Ottawa, we can expect very soon to see a new Portrait Gallery, a new site for the Canadian War Museum and a new Heritage Institute. In Toronto, expansions are planned at the Royal Ontario Museum, the Art Gallery of Ontario, the Gardiner Museum of Ceramic Arts and the National Ballet School, along with a new opera house and refurbishment of Roy Thomson Hall. New concert halls, theatres and opera houses are springing up all across the U.S., Europe and Asia.)

At the same time, many museums (including the National Gallery of Canada) are already offering worldwide access to their digitized collections, and a new international agency, the Art Museums Imaging Consortium, is devoted to the electronic sharing of collections and information from around the world. The Virtual Museum of Canada allows online visitors to explore various collections, "handle" ancient objects, play games, and create music on old instruments gathered from the diverse cultures of Canada. The National Arts Centre is working with the National Research Council to develop new broadband connections to young Canadians.

Similar developments are happening in the performing arts. The Kirov Opera broadcasts full-length performances on the Internet. Opera production itself is being revolutionized by miniaturized video technology, and as the sophistication of the technology intensifies so will the potential for dissemination—and the demand for artists' work.

It is important not to be dazzled by the new technologies or panicked by their potential. For all the delivery trickery, technology remains a tool. But it is a tool whose impact is so momentous it demands a manner of thinking not conceivable a generation ago. The traditional ways our artists have expressed themselves are by no means played out, but the delivery systems are likely to alter profoundly.

Trapped in the intensifying struggle for day-to-day survival, our major arts organizations might protest that they are hardly in a position to do long-term strategizing for such imagined change. But they have little option. There is no guarantee that these changes will be entirely beneficial to the arts. As a basic first step, however, it is essential that our cultural organizations and their boards of directors make themselves aware of the challenges, the risks and the implications, and prepare to come to terms with them. The long-term health of these organizations —even their survival—depends on it.

One-Stop Shopping?

GIVEN THE POTENTIAL of the new communications technologies, including undreamed-of distribution methods, we might begin to think—at least in conceptual terms—about new "national" organizations to stimulate creativity.

In terms of galleries and museums, for instance, what are the arguments for and against centralizing collections in one great supermuseum or—while we're at it—one great warehouse, where the technological resources needed to replicate art for mass distribution can be housed alongside the original works?

In the case of the performing arts, we might think about a centralized creation, production and training centre for each of the disciplines—a network of centres of creative excellence across the country. A Canadian Centre for New Media at Banff, for example. The Banff Centre is already a world leader in technological experiment; with more resources and a broadened mandate, it could become the focal point of new media experiment and production. Perhaps designed along the lines of the Cube, an experimental centre on the outskirts of Paris, it would be dedicated to digital culture, covering all aspects of multimedia training and offering courses in making art with the new technologies. Resident artists would explore new forms of artistic expression and share their discoveries with their colleagues and the general public.

Or what about a true national arts centre at the National Arts Centre? Equipped with the necessary technology and personnel, it could become the creation and distribution point for definitive theatrical or musical performance. Currently, one of the centre's strategic goals is to become a leader and innovator in the performing arts, and with the help of the National Research Council it uses new technologies for "virtual" rehearsals in the theatre and for arts education, with music director Pinchas Zukerman and theatre director Mardi Maraden conducting live intercontinental master classes and coaching sessions via broadband Web connections. The centre also produces classroom research materials and interactive outreach programming, and this could be an ideal base on which to build a full-scale research, development and production centre, linked to a national interactive creative network. Similar centres elsewhere might focus on research and creation in other art forms. Cross-disciplinarity would be encouraged, and the emphasis would be resolutely on fresh Canadian creativity being made readily accessible.

These production centres would function both as think-tanks and (with a funding process developed by federal and provincial ministries in partnership with such agencies as the CBC, Telefilm Canada and the Canada Council for the Arts) as centres for the commissioning and production of new work for presentation across the country. As the communications/delivery revolution intensifies, their concentration of expertise would also put Canada in an advantageous position internationally as a creator of accessible, high-quality art.

Centres like this would also help us come to terms with the problem of training. If Canadians are to equip ourselves effectively for the future, we must increase the availability of state-of-the-art professional training in arts and culture creation and presentation. These centres of creative excellence would function as high-intensity workshops or laboratories of ideas, facilitating individual and group experiment and developing a cadre of young professionals fully versed in the potential of new technological advances.

This plan need not (should not) involve a big bureaucracy. In terms of performance personnel, it could include a corps of performers for each discipline, called on to work as needed in a kind of repertory-theatre manner. Much of the work (and eventually production) would be Web-based. And each centre would be structured to ensure that regional autonomy was not undermined—in theatre, for example, artistic directors and playwrights from across Canada, and across Canada's cultures, would be included in the process. Nor would they work in a vacuum. They would be permanently linked, sharing resources and discoveries, working collaboratively to enrich the national cultural fabric.

It might be argued that, in an era of growing regionalization, it makes no sense to centralize in this way. Certainly, a program of this kind should not be developed at the expense of the local and the live. Audiences will always gravitate to the shared live experience. But it seems clearer and clearer that the new delivery systems will demand some kind of centralized production planning. And while it could also be argued that a central commissioning and distribution program (in theatre, for instance) might diminish attempts to establish local identity, such centralization would certainly improve the haphazard system of co-productions that exists across the professional Canadian theatre network. What should also not be forgotten are the glory days of CBC drama, when the network regularly commissioned, produced and broadcast theatre on a national basis. No one complained then that the regions were being undermined; indeed, it was one more means by which the regions could collectively get to know one another better.

Centralized production is an idea that goes far beyond the Net clips, catalogues, samplers and virtual tours that are already available to anyone connected to the Web. The elimination of touring costs (so long a convincing argument against taking shows of all kinds on the road); the costs of acquisition for museums, and of insurance (obviously lower if holdings can be circulated without leaving the building); reduced (or increased?) performer fees; the implications for unions; the possible diminution of the artist base; the reduction in performance opportunity: these are only the first issues, both positive and negative, that spring to mind when this kind of centralization is considered.

Art, Business and the New Technology

MONTREAL'S DANIEL LANGLOIS is a potent symbol of the synergy that can be created when business, technology and artistic creativity intersect. Internationally recognized as an innovator in the field of computer animation, Langlois has used the proceeds from his Softimage company, which specializes in advanced uses of digital technology for film (*Jurassic Park, Men in Black, Titanic, The Mask, Star Wars—The Phantom Menace*) to underwrite a series of enterprises aimed at giving concrete expression to his belief that the world of the arts, the world of the new technological sciences and the world of business need each other. The new digital technologies, he believes, must be used by artists not only to create marketable products, but also to pursue an ongoing critique of what we are doing to our lives— to engage, in other words, in the kind of cultural dialogue that has always dominated artistic expression.

Central to this philosophy is the notion that artists must be set free to follow their dreams. To enable this to happen, Langlois has created a wide-ranging network of interconnected companies. At the hub is Ex-Centris, a multiple theatre complex–cum–production centre in which independent producers and creators have access to digital technologies, blending a high-tech image research lab with a state-of-the-art presentation facility. His film production company, Media Principia, specializes in making movies using advanced digital technologies. He founded the Montreal International Festival of New Cinema and New Media to explore emerging genres and showcase independent films, video and new media. He has endowed research chairs at the University of Sherbrooke and Concordia University.

And, to support the ongoing experiment, his Daniel Langlois Foundation for Art, Science and Technology, founded in 1997, distributes about $500,000 a year in grants to artists exploring how the new technologies affect the way we live. Of the 15 projects chosen from an application list of 302 in 2002's international competition, 6 were from Canada, among them proposals from some of the country's most interesting experimenters. The foundation also operates a research and documentation centre, organizes conferences, and publishes papers on the interaction of art and science through technology.

By giving equal play to art, technology and business, Langlois's vision places the humanistic function of the artistic experience firmly at the centre of the modern world.

8

BUSINESS AND THE ARTS

Whenever I hear the world culture, I reach for my revolver.
— Commonly attributed to Hermann Goering, but actually a distortion
of a line from HANNS JOHST's 1933 play, *Schlageter*

Whenever I hear the word culture, I reach for my chequebook.
— JACK PALANCE, playing a film producer
in Jean-Luc Godard's *Le Mépris*

BUSINESS SUPPORT FOR cultural activity has been called, with some justification, capitalism with a conscience. The reinvestment of a portion of business profits in the community is widely recognized as an obligation of good corporate citizenry, and a recent survey showed that nine out of ten Canadians believe corporations should do more than simply make a profit. This belief has traditionally motivated substantial numbers of corporate philanthropists, who do their bit on arts boards across the country, volunteer advice, sign generous cheques and twist the arms of their fellow captains of industry at the club.

It is by no means simply a Canadian phenomenon. Many in the nation's cultural community, indeed, point across the border for examples of better practice. A century ago, as rail, steel and oil indus- tries and large-scale intercontinental immigration ushered in the modern world, a generation of inspirational U.S. philanthropists— Andrew Carnegie and John D. Rockefeller leading the way—set new standards for charitable giving. Their model, based sometimes on a simple belief in the value of art to society, sometimes on a sense of civic duty, has been industriously copied. The proportion of arts fund- ing that comes from the private and business sector in the U.S. has always been far higher than is common in Canada. This can be seen as linked to the comparatively low level of government help given to the cultural sector in the U.S., but the enormous tax write-offs allowed for arts donations can also be viewed as a balancing form of govern- ment subsidy, albeit administered through private patrons.

(Although the level of charitable giving in the U.S. has dropped in recent years, it is still substantial. If Canadians were as generous in their charitable donations as their neighbours to the south, Canadian charities would receive an extra $6 billion a year. If the arts received the same percentage of those charitable donations as they receive today, that would add $600 million a year to their coffers, or about five times the 2001–02 grants budget of the Canada Council for the Arts. In fact, at the end of the 1990s, as the economy suffered significant set- backs, corporate donations to the arts in Canada were dropping. In 1997, the arts accounted for 20 per cent of all corporate giving; two years later that had halved, to 10 per cent. However, the percentage has recently begun to rise again, primarily in Toronto, where the new building surge has encouraged the emergence of a small group of pace- setting big donors.)

In the ongoing discussion of business involvement with the arts, it is from time to time suggested that Canada should move towards the

U.S. system. It has even been suggested that Canada's arts groups should be encouraged to become entirely independent of public funding. This is dangerous ground. No one questions the need for arts and cultural groups to find more support from the private sector; business has an important role to play, and that role can be rewarded with important benefits. But to place the fortunes of our arts and culture sector at the mercy of organizations whose ultimate reckoning lies in the bottom line is to risk seeing the sector degenerate into market-dominated commercialism. Success in the market is not to be scorned; a hit show, a best-selling book, makes everyone happy. But market success is only part of what the arts are about.

IN THE MOST RECENT SURVEY carried out by the Council for Business and the Arts in Canada, the prime motivating factor Canadian businesses gave for their arts support was the belief that arts organizations improve the quality of life in communities, spark creativity and self-renewal, and encourage new thinking. The reasons Halifax grocery magnate and art collector Donald Sobey gave for creating a new $50,000 biennial prize for visual artists under forty provide an interesting example. He sees his new award as a way both to stimulate the discussion of contemporary art and to give an artist the chance to spend a year doing nothing but making art. Though his own tastes as a collector tend to the conservative, Sobey doesn't shy away from controversy; the finalist list for the first prize, awarded late in 2002, did not include a single painter.

Those philanthropists who do contribute to the arts seem increasingly prepared to stay involved for the long haul. Examples abound of substantial enlightened private subsidy, either in infrastructure or in art itself—Roy Thomson Hall in Toronto, the Chan Centre in Vancouver, the McCord Museum of Canadian History in Montreal, the Mendel Art Gallery in Saskatoon, the Glenbow Museum in Calgary, the Vincent Massey collection of English and Canadian art, the Henry

Birks collection of Canadian silver donated to the National Gallery of Canada, Phyllis Bronfman Lambert's continuing sustenance of the Canadian Centre for Architecture in Montreal and Walter Carsen's consistent underwriting of the repertoire of the National Ballet of Canada. Other examples come in the form of prizes named for their donors and richly endowed—among them the Molson, Giller and Griffin prizes and the new Sobey Art Award—and direct gifts, such as media magnate Ken Thomson's donation of $370 million in cash and artworks to the Art Gallery of Ontario and former Ontario lieutenant-governor Hal Jackman's gift of $15 million to the University of Toronto to underwrite liberal arts and humanities programs.

Of course, altruism is increasingly tempered, these days, by pragmatism. The charitable contributions that private business makes to cultural activities, in cash and in kind, can have as much to do with the desire for economic advantage as with the desire to do public good. Private sponsorship of specific events is often more a matter of product positioning than philanthropy; in some cases, corporations look on their investments in the cultural community not as charitable donations but as part of their communications or promotions budget. Public profile of a brand can be a long-term lucrative payoff, and it is hardly surprising that businesses like to attach their arts subsidies (and their name) to successful ventures with a positive public image. Businesses also know that associating themselves with creativity has a spinoff effect in terms of perception; implicit in the relationship is the idea that these are supporters with questioning and open minds.

Bell Canada has contributed to the Stratford Festival every year since its launch in 1952. By the festival's fiftieth anniversary, Bell's total giving to the festival had reached $1.5 million—a minor sum, perhaps, by comparison with large-corporation donations south of the border, but a significant figure by Canadian standards. In the early years, the help came in the form of production sponsorships. Later, the emphasis was placed on

joint marketing partnerships. "There are lots of good altruistic reasons"
why the company has stayed with the festival, says Bell's senior director of
sponsorships and corporate donations, Louise Bellingham. "But commer-
cialism is an important economic driver in the province. The audience
attracted to Stratford is highly educated, a good audience for the com-
pany. Stratford is a good partner, and with it you get brand recognition."

This kind of strategic underwriting, with sponsorships customized
to the donor, is a growing trend. Companies exist for the sole purpose
of creating these liaisons. (Since the Toronto chapter of the Association
of Fundraising Professionals was founded in 1994, its membership has
risen from 109 to 534, making it the fourth-largest chapter in North
America.) This strategy is also good competitive economics. A private
enterprise that can demonstrate a financial commitment to its community's creative life is distinguishing itself from its competitors and
proclaiming its rootedness in the place where it does business. It can
look like social responsibility, and that can pay invisible dividends.
Shareholders like it because it creates a favourable image in the minds
of consumers. It is an investment in the future.

Some of the most significant contributions to the Canadian cultural infrastructure have emerged from partnerships of this kind. The
Toronto-based international Four Seasons hotel chain has given $20
million to the new home for the Canadian Opera Company in Toronto
in exchange for naming rights: the Four Seasons Centre for the Performing Arts is expected to have a major impact on the international
music world. "To be frank," said Four Seasons Hotels Inc. chairman and
CEO Isadore Sharp about the company's commitment, "it's a commercial venture for us." Also in Toronto, Ed and David Mirvish have helped
transform downtown Toronto through an imaginative partnership that
involved the refurbishment of two theatres and the creation of 8,000
jobs. In Ottawa in 1997, Newbridge Networks and Le Groupe de la
Place Royale made dance history when they collaborated, with the

help of several telecommunications companies, on the first experiment in international choreography via computer. Dancers from Le Groupe performed before an audience at the Canadian Museum of Civilization in Ottawa. Simultaneously, in real time, dancers in Berlin accompanied them on a back-projected screen with the help of an interactive video link. When the performance was over, the audience was able to engage both sets of dancers in real-time discussion. At Toronto's Theatre Passe Muraille, a maker of backrests installed samples of its product in the theatre's notoriously uncomfortable bleacher seating.

The problem with one-off sponsorships is the fact that an ongoing relationship is rarely established, so the energy invested in making the contact and generating the deal has had only a short-term impact. Arts organizations are also finding that they must become increasingly creative if they hope to succeed in their head-to-head competition with sports groups and others seeking the ongoing corporate sponsorship dollar. What is being offered is direct, quid pro quo marketing, far removed from pure philanthropy, and if this makes the purists shudder, it also demonstrates the degree of gritty realism necessary for any arts organization to survive.

Managing the relationship between giver and getter can be a delicate matter, particularly in relation to "earmarked" giving, and the larger the gift, the more tact the balancing act is likely to require. It is vital that organizations matching donors to specific events make sure the match is right: corporations as well as individuals can be notoriously conservative when their names and reputations are attached to controversial work. Sponsors for musicals, comedies, the classics and the big-ticket specials are far easier to find. It is also important, however, that organizations receiving sponsorship support are able to retain full control over their activities. As recent events in the U.S. and England have shown, problems can arise when the line between organization and sponsor becomes blurred. The Metropolitan Opera, for instance, came into messy legal conflict in 2003 when it was charged with violating the terms of a donor's will that specified that the donated funds could only be used for "traditional" productions. However, pragmatism need not spell the end of integrity, on either side of the fence. Careful handling of sponsorship in an atmosphere of mutual trust allows businesses to maintain their ethical standards and at the same time act in their own interest, and allows arts organizations to increase their corporate support without compromising their central vision.

> *People hardly ever contribute because something needs something. They contribute because they want "the wonderful" to happen. The wonderful is not, say, the opera house, but the performances that will occur there, the magic among the artists and with the audience. It's the service you provide.*
> —DORY VANDERHOOF, cultural development consultant

Arts organizations are increasingly testing other possibilities for collaboration with the private sector, matching their needs to available corporate expertise. Corporations with a stake in the electronic future, for instance, could provide opportunities to tap new production methods or new markets that can only be reached electronically, or to facilitate programs of international exchange. Other innovations involve study scholarships, mentor programs, sabbatical funds and even dedicated incomes; some of the more imaginative donations in the U.S. have included land (in one case, oil was discovered beneath the donated property) and a sporting goods store that the recipient arts group was expected to run. Whatever the means, the intent is the same: to provide means to reinforce the resilience and quality of work of those who create for the non-profit sector.

Government can encourage these partnerships through strategic manipulation of its own support—incentive programs, for instance, where government funds are provided as long as private resources are also obtained, and matching grants. Matching grants can take various forms, including dedicated amounts from government that are released once an equivalent amount has been raised from other sources and reverse matches, where government agrees to match whatever amount is raised in private support.

The latter system raises an important and contentious issue, since government is allowing private decisions to influence public spending: in effect, a form of privatization of arts funding. If, for instance, an individual or a corporation donates $10,000 to a symphony orchestra under a matching grant program, a tax credit is received. Assuming a top tax bracket, that credit would amount to about 40 per cent, or $4,000, of forgone income to the government. That would make the actual cost to the donor $6,000, in exchange for which the donor has been able to influence $16,000 worth of arts spending.

In its role as facilitator, government should also make corporate involvement with culture more inviting. The whole area of federal tax policy, for instance, is worth serious review. Persistent lobbying from the cultural community, organized through the Canada Council for the Arts, resulted in an improvement in tax allowances for charitable contributions to non-profit arts organizations, but violinist Lara St. John is only one vociferous advocate among many urging a 100 per cent deduction, putting Canadian donors on a level playing field with those in the U.S. In addition, the House of Commons Standing Committee on Finance has recommended the removal of the 47 per cent capital gains tax on gifts such as stocks or real estate made to Canadian non-profit organizations. Tax changes could also create a more encouraging climate in which business could be steered in the direction of funding scholarships and specific cultural research projects—tangible, results-oriented investments that would add lustre to the name of the sponsoring donor.

Optimists argue that a more generous tax return on charitable donations would stimulate the country's business sector to move towards U.S.-style arts patronage. However, we must be cautious in our expectations. The principle of public support for culture in Canada is so well entrenched that there is no widespread perception of the need for large-scale private assistance. Tax breaks will help, but we should not expect a rapid turnaround.

Another government tool for encouraging private giving is the percentage for the arts system that is widely used in Canada and abroad. Under this scheme, corporations are required to invest part of their profits in the community. In some cities in North America, a percentage of the construction costs of new buildings (often government facilities) must be spent on artworks. In Russia, municipalities are required to spend a specified percentage of their budgets on arts and culture. In Sweden, a program has been introduced under which businesses are required to fund artistic experiences for their employees.

At the same time, the cultural community is coming to recognize that it must make itself as attractive as possible to the corporate culture. If Canadian businesses are indeed moving towards the idea of philanthropy as a long-term community investment, that commitment surely presupposes that there is an attainable end in sight—part of which is a healthy, accountable, stable, sustainable arts infrastructure. Active, accountable boards and efficient, effective management, properly overseen, are essential. And in that regard, the Council for Business and the Arts in Canada (CBAC), which works to bring arts organizations and business together in a mutually beneficial partnership, sees an increasing need for business leadership on arts organization boards. It is needed not only to provide help with management skills, but to help identify new ways to attract support from the business community. With intelligent safeguards on diversity of expression and a proper recognition of the unique nature of the non-profit arts enterprise, these moves might prove the catalyst for a coming-together of purpose that has the power to transform the way we live together.

How to Increase Corporate Allure:
A 12-Step Program for Arts Organizations

1   *Make value from your virtue.* Most arts organizations, forced to live tightly within their means, know how to make dollars stretch. Use the evidence of your balance sheets to show the leanness of your operations and how much is reinvested in your community.

2   *Ensure your fundraising targets and projects are as diverse as possible.* Go prospecting across the community. To keep the cash flowing, offer more opportunities to participate than a once-a-year gala pitch.

3   *Make sure the quid pro quo benefits you offer are substantial.* Value for money should be demonstrated at every turn. Benefits should be tailored to the donor's interests. In a CBAC survey, three of four respondents said they preferred specific sponsorships, and two in three said the most decisive factor was the appropriateness of the "fit" for their image.

4   *Pitch for the right reasons.* Covering a budget shortfall isn't one of them. To a businessperson not familiar with the arts world, that reads like questionable management. Stress, instead, the value of what you are doing in the community that you (and the business you are pitching) serve.

5   *Stay clear of social or emotional blackmail.* Your manager's family may be starving and your chairperson's house in hock, but it is not wise to overplay the notion of moral obligation. The best support partnerships are fair, win-win deals between equals.

6   *Demonstrate buy-in from government and other areas of the private sector.* Nothing inspires like example.

7   *Be realistic in the amounts requested and pitch projects that have a finite shape.* Ventures that can sustain themselves once the initial investment is made are attractive to donors from the results-oriented world of business.

8   *Take every chance available to improve business skills, governance techniques and money-management strategies.* Ambitious managers will do that as a matter of course. Boards should be involved as well. This imparts confidence.

9   *Pay attention to the new demographics.* Living up to its mandate "to promote an understanding and appreciation of the diversity of the cultural world," the Royal Ontario Museum decided to create a new South Asia gallery. Philanthropist-financier Christopher Ondaatje contributed half the $2-million cost; for the balance, the ROM made a direct appeal to Ontario's South Asian community. Within six weeks, the target was met. Money *is* available when potential donors are given the right reasons to contribute.

10   *Stay informed about business trends.* Being abreast of political and social issues conveys the impression of having a foot in the real world. It inspires confidence.

11   *Give the donor free tickets.* But request that the tickets are given not to the donor's staff (who tend to leave the seats empty) but to groups working with people with disabilities, people with low incomes and, if appropriate, young people. This increases the outreach effect for both the donor and the organization.

12   *Don't be afraid to stroke the donor.* Almost everyone appreciates public recognition. Be generous in your acknowledgement of other people's generosity.

Volunteerism

ARTS ORGANIZATIONS, like other Canadian charities and not-for-profit enterprises, are discovering that they can rely less and less on help from volunteers. Although volunteers still account for the equivalent of more than 500,000 full-time jobs, volunteerism in Canada dropped 31 per cent between 1997 and 2000. The generation of volunteers who helped build most of Canada's major arts institutions in the 1970s and 1980s, and who still carry much of the volunteer load, is moving into its senior years. As is the case in professional arts management, there is a growing concern about succession, particularly since the new generation of volunteers is being more choosy about what it supports.

Government is helping; $50 million was recently committed by Ottawa to the Canada Volunteerism Initiative, a five-year program aimed at promoting volunteerism and developing training programs. But arts organizations also have a role to play in attracting and keeping the often-crucial free help. Persuading supporters of the value of the enterprise should be at the forefront of their efforts; a 2000 study on giving and volunteering by the Canadian Centre for Philanthropy and Volunteer Canada showed "belief in the cause" as the prime motivation for volunteering. However, women also showed a strong tendency to want to use the experience as a way to explore their personal strengths—which can translate into wanting more involvement in the decision-making process.

At the Art Gallery of Ontario, for instance, the volunteer group, after long and unsatisfactory negotiations with management, withdrew its services in the summer of 2002. They formed their own support organization to allow them to run fundraising events in the way they chose and to direct the money they raised towards the purchase of contemporary art. While it is possible to sympathize with these ambitions, it is hard to endorse them. An arts organization's management is employed to run the place in a professional manner; it can hardly be expected to hand over decision-making in such areas as acquisition to a self-selected group of unpaid volunteers, however well intentioned. Nevertheless, it is increasingly clear that today's volunteers are not content to simply staff the gift shop, but—with donated time becoming a more and more precious commodity— want more of a say in how their skills are used and how the money raised is spent. Arts organizations must be flexible in finding ways to benefit from this source of goodwill without compromising their integrity. Giving volunteers a sense of involvement, letting them know that their contributions make a crucial difference, and giving them a chance to learn and grow through their involvement are all important factors in building a healthy volunteer community ... particularly since volunteers tend to become donors later in life.

III

MAKING
IT HAPPEN

9

THE ROLE OF
GOVERNMENT

---

*Arts and culture are not for the few. Cultural participation develops
our creativity, enriches our citizenship, feeds the spirit. Arts and culture
must be integrated into our lives and our communities. Arts and
heritage organizations must reach out to their communities. Build
partnerships with business and academia. Engage the young and
build audiences for the future.*

—Prime Minister JEAN CHRÉTIEN, announcing
the Tomorrow Starts Today federal investment
in arts and culture, May 2, 2001

In moments of crisis, only imagination is more important than knowledge.

—ALBERT EINSTEIN

THIS BOOK IS built on a belief in the paramount importance of
creative activity in the fulfilled human life, a conviction that
access to creative expression and the shared creative heritage
should be universal, and a commitment to creative excellence. Central to the entire exercise is the unyielding idea that, in a world where
profit and the bottom line assume a dangerous primacy, society has the
responsibility to provide long-term support for culture in all its
multiplicity: the making of it, the enjoyment of it and the sharing of it.
Since uncertainty underpins all creative enterprise, someone must be
prepared to underwrite the possibility of failure. That someone must

be society itself, in large part through the funding processes of government.

Public support for cultural activity has been decried as interventionist, and it is, but it is interventionist only in the sense that universal health care and education are interventionist, or that building roads and airports and buying helicopters for the military is interventionist. Cultural support provides money from the public purse for a social good: one of the essential services that society elects government to provide.

One of government's responsibilities is to help convince Canada's citizens (and its educators) that active involvement with our created living heritage is worth everyone's time. To do that, it must first be convinced itself. An awareness of these values should be rooted in the broad policies of government. We are far from this ideal at present. Although certain areas of government have been vocal in their advocacy of cultural values, we have far to go before a belief in those values permeates official thinking and action.

The first aim of any cultural policy is to allow every individual to develop a higher consciousness of their lives—to make citizens wiser and freer to make choices. —PIERRE JUNEAU

THE INVOLVEMENT of the Canadian people in funding arts and culture has a lengthy history. The Public Archives (now the National Archives) was established in 1872. The National Gallery of Canada was founded in 1880. As early as 1929, a royal commission was recommending the creation of a national broadcasting system; the Canadian Radio Broadcasting Commission was set up in 1932 and was replaced by CBC-Radio Canada in 1936. The following year the first Governor General's Literary Awards were distributed, and in 1939 the National Film Board was created. The Kingston Artists' Conference in 1941, a pan-Canadian gathering, marked the first time the artistic community had come together to speak with a unified voice about the need for official government recognition and support of the arts. Several years of escalating arts-community activism followed the end of the Second World War, as Canada came to terms with the challenges of social reconstruction, and in 1949 the government set up the Royal Commission on National Development in the Arts, Letters and Sciences. Its conclusions (commonly known as the Massey-Lévesque report, after its co-chairs) were published in 1951; among its 150 recommendations were the creation of the Canada Council and the National Library of Canada. The National Library Act was passed in 1953; four years later, the Canada Council came into being, funded by income on a $50-million endowment. Another burst of activity occurred in the 1960s, with the creation of the National Arts Centre (1966), Telefilm Canada and the Canadian Radio-television and Telecommunications Commission (both 1968).

In the decades since, the federal government and its agencies have built a countrywide network of support and distribution for Canada's creators, cultural organizations and cultural industries. Although few of Canada's provinces and territories have created ministries specifically responsible for culture, they all provide funds to support cultural activity, as do cities and municipalities across the country. By 2001–02, cultural spending by all governments in Canada amounted to $6.8 billion, with $3.2 billion (about 45 per cent) in federal money and $2.1 billion (30 per cent) coming from the provinces.

Too many of our arts organizations have—for too long—operated on a wing and a prayer. We want to help them become modern, viable organizations—ready, willing and able to thrive in the new economy.
    —Heritage Minister SHEILA COPPS, May 25, 2001

Despite the economic setbacks of the 1990s, the federal government maintained its commitment to creativity, and in May 2001,

Heritage Minister Sheila Copps and Prime Minister Jean Chrétien announced Tomorrow Starts Today, an additional three-year investment of $568 million in the arts and cultural industries. The program was extended for a further year late in 2003. The largest increase in federal funding for the arts in forty years, the new money was targeted at underwriting creativity, building audiences, maximizing access and developing private-sector partnerships.

These are all fine aims, and if they persuade the powerful to agree to put more money into culture, they should be trumpeted from the rooftops. But it would be misguided to make economic and social arguments the prime basis for arts support. This has been happening increasingly in Britain, a country whose arts policies helped shape Canada's early approaches, and we should be wary of following that path: not only are the benefits difficult to quantify, but undue stress on "deliverables" and "benchmarks" and other controls on public spending, along with requirements for "outreach" and "inclusion" if arts enterprises are to earn their subsidy, threaten to reduce them to mere instruments of social policy.

Their significance to society goes far deeper than that, although the argument that the value of art and culture cannot always be measured in the marketplace is, we have to admit, not necessarily a helpful one for bureaucrats. Demands for accountability and structural integrity—necessary as they are—all too often take the elastic out of bureaucracy's ability to respond. But in a period in which the borders of art-making are so porous, in which definitions are unstable, in which art, culture and heritage must fight for survival against the demands of the commercial world, it is essential—nowhere more so than at the outer edges of artistic creativity—that we maintain an embracing support structure and response system.

Conductor Herbert von Karajan was once asked by an American journalist what he did whenever one of his Salzburg Festival productions ran over budget. "I call Vienna," the maestro replied, "and the ministry sends more money."

That support can take the form of direct subsidy, or it can come from measures such as content rulings, quotas, tariff barriers or even (in the case of cultural industries such as publishing and broadcasting) ownership restrictions. In Canada, we have evolved a complex mix of these approaches, one that is constantly undergoing revision and refinement. Whatever the approach, culture transcends ideology and political dogma. It is in the interests of the nation to ensure that every citizen is given the opportunity to develop in the areas of creative thinking, ethical judgement and the exercise of the imagination.

A recognition and endorsement of that significance is what must be integrated into the daily business of government ministries and agencies at every level. All ministers and ministries, not merely those with an interest in culture and the arts, should undertake active advocacy, promoting the idea of the arts and culture as a social and personal good and working to encourage social participation. Foreign affairs, health and welfare, finance, environment, immigration, aboriginal affairs— they all have a role to play and a voice to contribute to the long-term validation of involvement with culture.

We might go further. Would it be beyond possibility for the federal cabinet to adopt a basic statement of principle affirming the importance of the arts and culture to Canadian society—much as we might affirm the central significance of defence or health—and requiring decision-makers in government to consider the cultural implications of their policies and spending as a routine element of their decision-making process?

When culture becomes part of everyday government discourse in this way, we will make serious steps towards public ownership. Everything connects. Federal support encourages non-governmental partners to become involved. Where government goes, the private sector tends to follow, so government advocacy of cultural activity will help persuade other important players—foundations, both private and public, as well as the business sector—of the importance of these initiatives.

In that regard, a proposal made by University of British Columbia president Martha Piper, in her 2002 Killam Annual Lecture, merits serious consideration. She called for the creation of a human sciences advisory body to the prime minister, similar to the Prime Minister's Advisory Council on Science and Technology. The function of what she calls the Prime Minister's Advisory Council on a Civil Society would be to "advise the government on the measures needed to be taken to move Canada closer to the ideal of a civil society"—which she defines as "a vigorous citizenry engaged in the culture and politics of a free society." She suggests the agency be composed of "leaders in humanities and social science research, creative and performing arts, business, industry and labour." This is an inspired way to root the discussion of challenging concepts deeply within the governing bureaucracy, while also providing an ideal opportunity to make them accessible to a broad swath of Canadian society, and it is a proposal that the cultural community should pursue with urgency.

Government funding for arts and culture in Canada is currently drawn directly from tax revenues. A number of the alternatives that exist in other countries have been widely discussed (and in some cases advocated) here.

In England a dedicated state lottery raised multiple millions of pounds, much of which went to strengthening the cultural infrastructure, particularly new and existing buildings.

In some countries, arts funding is raised through dedicated taxes, often in the form of a sales tax. Movie ticket surcharges, for example, are imposed in France (where film producers can reclaim the gathered funds as long as the money is spent on a new French film) and in Argentina (where the surcharge is used to help fund not only the movie industry, but libraries and the general arts community).

Developing the Palate

The only way to grow an artistic community is to grant it an unfettered, open environment where artists do not cower in fear of losing corporate dollars should their work fall outside the mainstream.

——GARTH DRABINSKY, TEDCity conference, Toronto, June 2000

MAKING DECISIONS ABOUT what we like and do not like in new art—in any art, for that matter—is never easy. It involves the development of a critical sense, some awareness of the artwork's context, its background and its intent. It can be tempting to disparage, to ridicule without understanding, to damn with faint praise. But we have a responsibility to give art its place. That means taking what critics have to tell us with a grain of salt, making our own decisions, doing the work that lets us reach those informed positions. None of it need be onerous; indeed, it can be a journey of discovery that is both enlightening and enriching. If a work of art has the possibility of being interesting, then we should give it the dignity of meeting it on its own terms. Self-censorship is the worst kind of trap; we may well be cutting ourselves off from an imaginative adventure that could change our lives. Learning about art is like, as the novelist and essayist Jeanette Winterson once said, learning about wine. The only way to develop a palate is to drink it.

That brings us again to education, in its broadest sense. To banish the insecurity so many people feel around new art, to encourage a closer, more intelligent relationship between artist and audience, and thus to render both art and audience far less susceptible to the charlatans, we need to develop an audience able to discriminate.

In our eagerness to equip our new generations with the right technological tools, we have shamefully neglected the humanities, and it is time to bridge the gap that separates the academic world of literature, history and ethics from the world of those outside the academy. But education in the humanities and liberal arts should not be confined to the young. It is a lifelong process: it develops the faculty for examining ideas that lies at the basis of democracy. A solid familiarity with cultural exploration and inquiry throughout humankind's history is an essential element in a rounded, contributing individual. It provides us with the context to evaluate the society in which we live.

The task of bridging this gap is one that might be taken on by a coalition of Crown corporations such as the SSHRC and the Canada Council for the Arts, think-tank agencies such as the Canadian Commission for UNESCO and the Council of Ministers of Education of Canada, and non-governmental organizations such as the Canadian Conference of the Arts, bringing together the best of Canada's intellectual resources to form a united front of imagination and ideas.

Part of what is needed is sustained advocacy, and it is in the area of advocacy that the arts and culture community can find common cause with government. This will involve more than well-intentioned op-ed pitches for support written by artistic directors, useful as those are. One possibility would be a national Arts Awareness campaign, pitched towards advocacy without condescension, highlighting the range and availability of arts and cultural events, with localized brochures linked to some kind of ticket discounting. Or perhaps it is time for something bolder—as proposed earlier, something along the lines of the federal government's ParticipAction campaign. Personal health goes far beyond the improvement of individual life experience; it can also be calculated as a significant economic benefit in terms of reduced expectations of hospital and other health costs. In the same way, a campaign to put the arts and culture at the

centre of the social agenda will deliver benefits far beyond positioning more posteriors on the plush.

Any campaign of this kind must go hand in hand with renewed
efforts to make the experience of arts and culture more widely available. A fine example is World Poetry Day. One might assume, from the
sales reported by poetry publishers, that this would be a specialist
event, drawing the committed but hardly striking a populist chord. In
fact, the reverse has proven to be the case; programs of international
readings in Ottawa draw turnaway crowds in larger numbers each
year.

The creation of a network of community cultural associations,
along the lines of the amateur soccer associations found across Canada,
is another possibility. This could be supplemented by a national network of reading and appreciation clubs, both live and virtual, structured for maximum community involvement, with a strong grassroots
focus. The key here is networking: the effect that one association can
have in its own community can be magnified many times through
sharing experiences and ideas across the nation.

The media should also be encouraged to play its part. The popular
media is always, it seems, willing to give some backbench oppor-
tunist the chance to become the latest voice of affront at this or that
artist's apparent insult to perceived popular morality. It is far less
comfortable engaging in serious, accessible discussion of the issues
the arts raise. To stimulate debate on cultural policy, we need an
ongoing campaign to develop thoughtful cultural journalism. This
would include education in critical writing, scholarships, internship
programs, seminars and other learning tools, perhaps along the lines
of the National Arts Journalism Program at Columbia University,
which gives arts critics, reporters and editors a nine-month sabbatical
to study, attend cultural events, and meet people from across the
spectrum of arts and entertainment.

Above all, it is vital that the cultural community's approach is positive and embracing. Whining won't work. What is necessary is a lively voice that can persuade its listeners that new and better ways of doing things are possible.

Equity and Cultural Diversity

MULTICULTURALISM IS A much-abused term. Its implications of social justice and equity have been used in some quarters—particularly education and public service—to force a quota-driven imposition of equality, attracting charges of political correctness and agenda-based politics. As well, the federal government policies of the 1970s and 1980s that encouraged immigrant peoples to retain their parent culture in their new land have been widely attacked as misguided. In the words of the writer Neil Bissoondath, an ardent opponent of official Canadian multiculturalism, those policies were built "on a basic lie—the refusal to acknowledge that the act of immigration changes you profoundly." Rather than allowing immigrants to become part of the society around them, he argues, multiculturalism turns ethnic communities into "museums of exoticism."

The act of immigration does change the individual profoundly; immigrants often make the most vocal advocates for the nation they adopt. This is one more reason all segments of the populace must be given the opportunity to be involved in cultural activities they find relevant and enjoyable. In developing an awareness of the diversity of cultural expression within our national boundaries, and a respect for that diversity, we take another step towards mutual understanding and goodwill. A commitment to cultural diversity implies a willingness to think beyond borders, to be open to alternative ways of imagining our lives together, and to allow many different visions equal play in the society we create.

The great law of culture is: Let each become all that he was created capable of being. —THOMAS CARLYLE

As Canada's diversity broadens, we gain more understanding of the importance of traditional and folk arts, and programs that protect and display this kind of cultural expression take on a fresh importance. These programs should include not only the celebration of this heritage through performance, scholarships and awards, but also its documentation, its transmission and teaching, and its preservation. What we have made in the past lets us know where we came from, both artistically and as a people. There is room on our stages, at our festivals and in our galleries both for the celebration of what has gone before and for what we are making afresh.

If assertions of the importance of cultural diversity are to be credible, the diversity of Canadian society must also be reflected in the makeup of government agencies and of arts organizations. They must look like the community they serve. The Canada Council's record of equity and diversity within its organizational structure is one for other organizations to emulate, but more needs to be done. Diversity on a peer assessment panel, for instance, means more than simply adding a person of colour to the group. Care must be taken to ensure that jury members bring to their work an informed understanding of diverse art forms and traditional and immigrant cultures.

Not all existing organizations find it easy to broaden their programming in this manner, and it is important not to force them to go unnaturally beyond their mandate. And if government wishes to take its endorsement of the importance of aboriginal and diverse cultures beyond the rhetorical, new resources will be necessary—to finance the addition of new organizations to the roster of producers and creators funded by the Canada Council and to underwrite the creation of innovative programs that promote the interaction of different cultures and make the cultural expression of minority cultures available to all Canadians.

The CanCon Question

THE ASTONISHING CULTURAL MIX of Canada today forces us to reconsider what we mean by the term "Canadian" (once such a comfortably monolithic notion). Meanwhile, the forces of globalization consistently destabilize and dissolve international borders. No wonder we rally our friends around the flag of cultural diversity. Facing the threat of international cultural uniformity (what has been called the "CocaCola-ization of the world"), we protect individual cultural expression every way we can.

Canadians clearly cherish a specific Canada: a Canada they can celebrate. For evidence, look at the annual race for the Stanley Cup, or the biennial Olympics, or the quadrennial Commonwealth Games: Canadian achievement becomes a way of asserting the Canadian identity. Yes, Canadians consume mass-market TV and movies in the same way Americans do. We do the same with cornflakes and tampons and home-repair equipment, and there is no reason why we should not. But that is not the issue, whatever the cultural free-traders will tell you. These are all elements of the mass marketplace.

The issue is the authenticity of the idea of Canada, which rests in the books Canadians are able to read, the music they are able to make, the TV and film they are able to watch. It has to do with what the bureaucrats and politicians call "creative capital"—the ability of Canadians to write those books and make those films, to create and innovate. Ideally, what should emerge from this environment is work that is intelligent, truthful and skeptical, work free to shine a uniquely Canadian light on the issues of the day. Quality must be given fair opportunity to find its place.

This is not as easy as it might seem. Canada is one of the world's largest per capita consumers of imported cultural goods, and it is likely to remain so. But because we have more geography than population, it can be difficult for Canadian cultural producers to establish a presence here. We lack the opportunities to use economies of scale. To make an hour of television drama in Canada, for instance, costs about ten times as much as it does to buy an hour of drama from the U.S. networks.

Much of the current health of Canadian culture is tied to a complex network of protective regulations and controls, built on the idea of levelling the playing field for Canadian creators. The CRTC; the Canadian Television Fund; tax credits; licensing requirements; ownership rules; significant investments in CBC-Radio Canada, the National Film Board and Telefilm Canada: these are all ways to ensure that the voices of Canada's artists continue to be heard. Despite regular calls from free marketeers for a loosening of these restraints, Canada is not the only country to find such measures necessary. France, Germany, Italy, the United Kingdom, Norway, Finland, the Netherlands and Australia, among many others, operate a variety of initiatives designed to enable their creators to flourish.

Internationally, Canada's protective measures have come under attack and legal challenge, with repeated demands for the removal of anything smacking of foreign ownership barriers or Canadian content quotas. In Canada, the opponents argue that it is pointless to hope regulation will reinforce our cultural identity in the face of the U.S. overspill, because the much-feared cultural integration has already occurred. What exists is a *North American* audiovisual industry, where the point of origin of a TV drama or a movie is of no significance.

In fact, in all the areas where distribution is controlled, the Canadian industry has been able to achieve reasonable, sometimes good visibility. Although imported music, imported TV shows and

imported films dominate our media, the protection of indigenous creativity has allowed the development of a Canadian voice that tells
Canadian stories. After four decades of nurturing, Canadian literature
is an international success. Canadian television programming is 39 per
cent Canadian-made (30 per cent in English, 65 per cent in French);
Canadian TV production won ten Emmy awards in 2002. Without
CanCon radio quotas, the Barenaked Ladies and Great Big Sea—just
two of many examples—would probably not have received the air-
time that led to their stardom.

Free-trade advocates also argue that the protection of cultural
industries, with rules that limit foreign ownership and impose levels
of Canadian content, shortchange consumers by keeping foreign competition out, thus limiting both choice (for Canadians) and the ability
to compete. If Canadian businesses were forced to compete in the
international marketplace, goes this argument, the ultimate beneficiaries would be Canadian consumers. Others see the CRTC's Canadian
content rules for radio as a form of indirect subsidy for the Canadian
music industry. They claim the rules not only create an artificial
demand for Canadian recordings but also encourage Canadians to tune
in to U.S. stations to hear the music they prefer.

It is a bittersweet truth that the corporate beneficiaries of this
Canadian protectionism often turn out to be foreign. Only 10 per cent
of the Canadian music industry is owned by Canadian firms, and both
the Barenaked Ladies and Great Big Sea are AOL–Time Warner artists.
Many of Canada's leading authors are published by branch plants of
foreign firms. And producers of television in Canada still must con-
tend with a lack of audiences; despite sustained investment in the sector by the federal government ($1.4 million a year), English-speaking
Canadians prefer to watch U.S. imports; only one Canadian-made
program, *Hockey Night in Canada,* ranks among the twenty most popular programs in English Canada. (In Quebec, on the other hand, all
ten of the top programs are made in Canada—a clear benefit of lin-

guistic distinctiveness.) This has led Telefilm Canada executive director
Richard Stursberg to consider bringing in new regulations demanding
a commitment to better promotion, marketing and audience-building
as a condition of funding.

We have left the theatrical market, unlike television, to its own devices.
This is a little like trying to fill a bathtub with the drain open.

— JACQUES BENSIMON, government film
commissioner and NFB chairperson

In the one area where Canada has no control over distribution—
movies—Canadian visibility is negligible. While Canadians indefatiga-
bly continue to produce fine films, many of them award-winning,
these films are seen more often by people on the festival circuit outside Canada than by Canadians. The Canadian share of the Canadian
box office is about 1.4 per cent overall (0.2 per cent in English, 9.8 per
cent in French), and the industry functions primarily as a supplier of
content for the American market—though even this function is hotly
contested by Hollywood interests.

Public subsidy and regulation are important tools, but should not
be looked on as sole solutions. Public subsidy exists at the whim of
politicians, not all of whom are equally convinced of its importance,
as witness Finance Minister John Manley's decision early in 2003 to
trim $25 million, or 25 per cent, from the government's contribution
to the Canadian Television Fund and at the same time to increase tax
credits for foreign producers on Canadian labour costs to 16 per cent
from 11 per cent.

Government aid should be reinforced by initiatives from the private sector—for instance, alternative distribution networks for Canadian films and a more aggressive approach to marketing and
promotion. In our mainstream movie houses, we could regularly feature short attractions before the main event—in the form of new

works by young Canadian filmmakers that have been paid for by the Canadian taxpayer. The movie chains would no doubt protest that such a policy would cut into the screen time available for them to sell, but perhaps it is time for quid pro quo legislation to ensure that promising Canadian work is made available to the general audience alongside the mass of material imported from Hollywood.

The CBC has a bold role to play in advancing the cause of Canadian culture: not only a role, we might argue, pointing to its substantial subsidy from the public purse, but an obligation. It has no business at all in competing with the popular market, either in television or in radio; indeed, private broadcasters are not out of place when they label CBC's incursions into the marketplace as unfairly subsidized competition. Any attempt to measure the CBC's effectiveness by market-based standards of listenership or viewership is misguided. The CBC's obligation is to reflect Canadian voices from every corner of the land, but its national reach also gives it the responsibility to bring the national cultural debate to Canadians. This is not something commercial broadcasters are likely to undertake, because it is not an area that promises profitable returns. But it is through the CBC, with its basis of public money, that the central debates about Canada's future and our ceaselessly changing cultural identity can be aired. Books, films, plays, dances, new media: all provide the materials from which argument, analysis and speculation can be shaped. Much more room should be made for them on the national broadcaster—and more resources (as well as redirected resources within the corporation) should be made available to make that possible.

Canadian content rules make sense as long as they are mechanisms for supporting Canadian creativity (though a case can be made for centralizing decision-making about what qualifies as Canadian content: currently, TV and film producers have to satisfy a quartet of regulatory bodies before their projects can be certified for funding). However, it is a misguided jump from this to the assumption that the Canadian culture supported should be devoted solely to matters Canadian. On the basis of that argument, Canada's government insisted for years that short films and documentaries seeking production help from the public purse should feature Canadian themes and locales.

Cultural nationalism and cultural freedom are different animals. The key to a flourishing creative identity for Canada lies in the freedom of our artists to create in whatever ways they think fit—and it is this freedom that should be protected by our legislators. Canadian creativity is an integral ingredient of our identity, an anchor of self-knowledge in a fluid world. But its Canadianness lies only in the fact that it is the creativity of Canadians; and that is the only prerequisite that can legitimately be imposed. Beyond that, all options are open. Canadian music is music made by Canadians. Canadian books are books written by Canadians—displaying what George Woodcock called "the restless variegation of a mature literature." *The Life of Pi*—a story of a young East Indian male shipwrecked en route to Canada and cast adrift in a lifeboat with only a Bengal tiger for company—is as much a Canadian novel as *Who Has Seen the Wind*. To properly protect our culture, it is excellence in creativity that should be supported, not nationalism. Take care of the creators, and the culture takes care of itself.

The Virtual World

THE INTERNET AND THE World Wide Web are beginning to transform the way society receives its cultural diet. We have embraced the new technologies, as a society, with alacrity and gusto. According to Statistics Canada, an estimated 7.2 million households (60 per cent of all households in Canada) had at least one member who used the Internet regularly in 2001. Nine out of ten young Canadians between 15 and 19 years of age use the Internet.

But we must be aware of what we are embracing. For all their potential for good, the advances we are seeing in the new communications technologies carry a heavy threat—both for individuals and for society.

One is social dissociation. When everything is available from the comfort of home, what is there to tempt us to go beyond our doors? The culture of cyberspace, while it demands new definitions of the real and the available, has immense seductiveness, and wholesale withdrawal from social participation is a significant threat.

Another is the Britney factor—the immediate and widespread electronic distribution of a standardized cultural product designed to appeal to the widest range of consumers. Its success, far greater than the most sophisticated conventional sales campaigns of Hollywood and the music industry (both industries have hastily co-opted the techniques), is reflected in the astronomic bankability of today's celebrities.

A third threat, perhaps more important to this book's theme, is the way the virtual world lessens the value of the reflective life. Today's communications technologies are so fast, and the amount of information to which they connect us is so great, that the sheer acquisition of knowledge crowds out the search for wisdom. There is no time for the intelligent filtering of that knowledge through experience and reflection.

So although we know the new technology is only the latest in a continuum of technologies for learning that includes books, blackboards, radio, film and video, the way we as a society choose to use this shiny new tool is one of the most interesting conundrums of the new millennium. We can, if we choose, fall into the trap of technological determinism, letting the tool itself dictate our responses in the haphazard way the global society allowed the World Wide Web to happen. Or we can grasp the tool and use it to help shape and express a distinctive cultural identity.

Imagination and innovation will be the international currency of the twenty-first century, and the Internet is where they will be bartered. Everyone has always had the opportunity to be an artist, of course, but the ability to present the created product to a global audience is entirely new. Anyone looking for a means of creative expression has immediate access, via the Internet, to distribution—of books, drawings, photographs, paintings—on a limitless scale. And none of this material needs to go through the traditional filter of evaluation. No jury citation or stamp of approval is necessary. You make it, you post it, it's there.

> One of the most advanced and innovative media arts communities in the world is located in Igloolik, a community of 1,200 beside the Arctic Ocean in the territory of Nunavut. Three interconnected groups—Igloolik Isuma Productions, Arnait (the Women's Video Workshop) and the Taraksuk Video Centre—share a studio and production centre.

Currently, only 5 per cent of the world's websites are Canadian; more than 70 per cent are American. And research shows that several of the websites and portals most visited by Canadians (often foreign websites) contain a minimal amount of Canadian cultural content. In positioning Canadian creativity globally via the Internet, Canadian artists have a vital role to play, and government has a responsibility to provide the necessary technological tools. The potential exists to create a far more diverse audience for art and culture than we have ever known. But we must ensure that the delivery systems of the future are available to all.

Already, Canada, which put the first geostationary communications satellite into orbit, has begun to invest substantially in the digitization of key existing cultural and historical materials to make them available for the new methods of distribution. As this trend intensifies, more and more raw materials will be needed to satisfy the global demand. The National Film Board of Canada makes its extensive film archive available to educational institutions via Internet broadband,

and the National Gallery of Canada and the Museum of Civilization both offer online educational tools and search engines.

> *An early contribution to research into new approaches to the design and delivery of Canadian cultural expression was the Canadian Creative Initiative. Started in the late 1990s, it brought together Stentor Communications, the Banff Centre and the Canada Council for the Arts in a partnership that enabled artists to develop skills in creating works in new media, such as live-networked events, interactive television and Web art.*

The federal Canadian Culture Online Program (CCOP) aims to promote a deeper understanding of Canadian culture through building digital cultural content and at the same time increasing audiences for that content. It intends to work with a broad range of partners to extend access to materials and to engage Canadians in contributing to the store of resources: in other words, to provide a gateway to Canadian culture online.

When it is complete, CCOP hopes to provide a seamless, user-friendly environment for exploration of the great wealth of Canada's culture and heritage. Libraries, archives and cultural institutions as well as private businesses and individual artists are involved in providing materials for segments such as "Canadian Memory," "Canadian Works of Reference" and the "Virtual Museum of Canada." An amount of $108 million was allocated in 2001 to underwrite the three-year second phase of the program's development. Several segments are already up and running; it is possible to access gallery exhibitions from various parts of the country, visit a variety of museums, obtain detailed information from various cultural agencies, and make links to *The Canadian Encyclopedia* and the National Archives. Other programs include the Canadian Cultural Observatory (www.culturescope.ca), which centralizes information on cultural activity throughout Canada and abroad, and connects Canadians working in cultural policy development.

Among the logical next steps to contemplate might be the creation, from this growing mass of available materials, of a free and universal cultural studies network that would be dedicated to raising the level of public involvement with the arts and culture, finding new ways to engage existing audiences, and developing new ways to reach new audiences, particularly in Canada's aboriginal and minority cultures. Linked to that could be a project devoted to stimulating innovative thinking by Canadians, in a forum and a climate designed for maximum openness and participation. Here are some preliminary thoughts on how they might be structured.

The Cultural Studies Network

JUST AS AN INFORMED CITIZENRY is crucial to the proper functioning of a democracy, so is an informed audience crucial to the health of a society's culture. In the Scandinavian countries, "civic literacy" is an important element of public participation in political debate. More than half the adults in Sweden are enrolled in adult education study circles, many organized by workers' groups. The opportunity exists for Canada to establish a national program of cultural literacy along similar lines.

Much of this aspect of a cultural studies network could be conducted via television and the Internet, with the CCOP as its information and access base; costs would be low, and access would be immediate for any Canadian with a Web connection. Individual research of this kind is already possible. But the network would also take tangible form, anchored by ongoing workshops and study groups in cities and towns across the country, organized locally and tailored to the interests and needs of individual communities. (One novel suggestion brought forward by former UNESCO director general Federico Mayor is the creation of a cultural security system that would, in the manner of a social security system, guarantee certain rights and protections The system would ensure that all members of society have access to the necessary tools for participation—that is, access to both infrastructure, such as e-mail and databases, and to life-long learning systems.)

Crucial to the network's functioning would be the collaborative involvement of Canada's arts agencies, already deeply committed to the CCOP. The National Arts Centre, for instance, has initiated a number of educational and outreach activities, designed to enhance its "national" role, that would fit this scheme. The Canada Council for the Arts has many years of experience in supporting grassroots activities of this kind. Funding shortages have prevented both agencies from realizing the full promise of these schemes.

Both "virtually" and in reality, the network would offer demonstrations and discussions led by creators, performers, administrators, critics and other professionals from the arts community, along with formal courses on such topics as theatre history and literary criticism. Television production companies, particularly those with a record of distance learning, would be encouraged to participate. Some presentations would be formal in structure, taped and downloadable for convenient viewing; some would be free-form, tied to issues of the day and taking place in real time to allow interaction with "student" audiences. Museums and community centres would be an integral part of the network. Conceivably, universities could play an anchor role as virtual coordinators for this community outreach.

Individuals absorb information from many sources, in many ways, and it is important to recognize that no one-size-fits-all system or curriculum exists for cultural education. Studies of distance-learning programs, for instance, have shown that students prefer to read assigned books as books, rather than as downloaded computer files. At the same time, higher education institutions in Canada place increasing reliance on websites, e-learning software and Web-based instructional tools, and these tools are likely to play an even greater role in course delivery in the future. Judiciously and intelligently developed, with an emphasis on interactivity, online technology can play a significant role in developing cultural literacy in Canada.

Throughout, the emphasis would be on accessibility of information, sharing of views and discussion. Proper attention would of necessity be paid to the complicated question of intellectual property and copyright in cyberspace. Eventually, along with the massive archive of information that is already being built, access to distance learning about the arts and culture of Canada, in all this richness and diversity, would be a free, guaranteed benefit of citizenship.

Already, significant funding under the CCOP goes to museums, archives and other agencies for the creation of digitized content for the CCOP website. But this deals primarily with content that already exists in other forms. The facilitation of original creativity should be a separate function of the website, allowing Canadians of all interests and backgrounds to interact with the creative community and the expressive potential of the new media. Properly administered, genuinely rooted in society, this is an initiative with the potential to transform the way we see ourselves, as individuals and as a nation. Not only does it neutralize the crushing challenge of Canada's geography, it transforms the rhetoric of cultural democracy into reality. It is in the interplay of our artists and our citizens that we will discover the blueprint for the Canada of tomorrow.

Making Room

ACCESSIBILITY HAS ALWAYS been a key factor in federal cultural policy—in terms of both physical location and affordability. It was a belief in the need to make cultural experiences available to the maximum number of Canadians that drove the flurry of building in the 1960s and 1970s: theatres, concert halls, galleries and museums sprang up across the country.

Even so, we find ourselves desperately short of adequate spaces in which to make the works of Canada's artists available to Canadians. Many of the buildings of three decades ago are showing their age and their functional limitations. And while much expansion, refurbishment and new building are scheduled, the revolution in communications and performance delivery suggests both the need and the opportunity to make better use of traditional spaces.

Flexible forms of exhibition space for the arts—venues that are home to all forms of music, dance, theatre and video art—are not new. One of the earliest examples is the Vancouver East Cultural Centre, a former church that is now a lively focus of activity for both its immediate community and the city's modern-dance and music scene. It is currently undergoing an expansion and refurbishment with $1 million of seed money from Vancouver City Savings Credit Union. Similar multifocal venues can be found in most cities across Canada.

However, consideration should be given to the imaginative use not only of libraries, community centres, theatres, art galleries, museums and concert halls, but of Canada's heritage buildings and monuments. Here as everywhere, human beings have created symbols of permanence—legacies that endure and tell something of the story of those who came before. If the organizations operating these sites are willing to go beyond a conventional concept of their use (perhaps with the help of volunteers), much opportunity exists to place artistic creativity at the heart of the community.

This built heritage ranges from something as obvious as Vancouver's venerable Orpheum Theatre (now the beautifully converted home of the Vancouver Symphony Orchestra) to something as inspired as a Maritimes church dating from the time of the Underground Railroad and now preserved by its parishioners. Buildings with Canada's history embedded in their bricks and beams can be found across the country, and new initiatives should go far beyond the merely preservative. Much of Canada's built heritage, with its diversity of references to colourful stories, its stylistic distinctiveness and the stability implicit in its survival, lends itself to imaginative reuse in urban development. Turning heritage structures and sites into centres for cultural activity is only the most obvious approach; the careful integration of these structures into evolving cityscapes will add vitality and cultural resonance to urban planning, and could lead to intriguing collaborations between designers and conservation experts.

In many places, time is of the essence. Over 20 per cent of Canada's built heritage has been lost in the past two decades alone, and one of the obligations of government is the preservation and maintenance of what remains. Measures are already in place to encourage Canadians to take a hand in this task; federal funds act as a lever to bring in players from different areas of government and from the private sector, and to encourage planners and heritage groups to find ways to integrate our built heritage into our daily lives. Opportunities for performance and presentation should be a prime consideration in this process.

Decentralization

STRIKING THE RIGHT BALANCE in government support for culture is a delicate matter. While many individuals involved in Canada's cultural community, particularly the cultural industries, expect direct intervention from Ottawa in matters such as Canadian content, copyright and access to markets, a strong desire also exists for greater autonomy at the local level.

Clearly, some things can be done only by the federal government and should remain in Ottawa's hands. International agreements and national protective legislation are high on that list. So is the provision of adequate funding and appropriate programs for the existing and emerging cultural community. The variations in cultural policies in different parts of Canada, and the sometimes piecemeal support that results, make it clear that centralized leadership in that area, too, is desirable.

Even so, support for the arts and culture can never be the preserve of a single level of government. Provincial, territorial and municipal governments all play a crucial role in demonstrating public commitment to the arts, culture and heritage. They contribute also to establishing an agreed-upon vision of the direction in which that support should go and how it should be provided. Even within a single level of government, multiple departments share responsibility for the implementation of cultural policy.

Cultural support fluctuates considerably among the provinces, but the province of Quebec, in particular, provides a model of effective, visionary assistance. In sound recording alone, Quebec provides more than 80 per cent of all provincial subsidies. The Conseil des arts et lettres du Québec gets $70 million a year from the province to put into arts support; the Ontario Arts Council gets barely a third of that, $24 million. A strong argument can be made for a far greater commitment to the support of cultural activity by all governments outside Ottawa. Although provincial and municipal governments invested $3.9 billion in culture in 2001–02 (57 per cent of the national total), 43 per cent of provincial cultural budgets was spent on libraries and heritage resources.

If provincial and municipal governments were to make a larger financial commitment to arts education, performing arts and visual arts, they would reinforce what is already a compelling case for the devolution of control over some cultural resources and programs to the local level. Centralized policy-making does not always take location into account, yet location is part of what defines culture. The creative aesthetic of the West Coast is quite different from the creative aesthetic of, say, Quebec, but a keen—or even appropriate—awareness of those differences is not always apparent in national funding decisions. This is not a matter of national party politics, as some might try to present it; it is a matter, rather, of a proper understanding of what drives the cultural creativity and identity of a region.

This principle seems well understood in the media industries. The CBC, the National Film Board, Telefilm Canada and the CRTC all maintain regional offices with various levels of autonomy. The Canada Council for the Arts flirted with the idea more than a decade ago, placing an office in the Atlantic region, but closed the office on grounds of economy when budgets grew tight. (Its board also debated opening one on the West Coast, but never followed through. These initiatives were intended, in any case, more as centres of information and visible presence than as direct sources of financial help.)

But the arguments for the decentralization of funding decision-making, as well as the local/regional administration of the programs within which the money is spent, demand a serious second look. It is at the local level, after all, that we most clearly see the challenges, the tensions and the opportunities of cultural activity. It is at the local level that we can obtain the best-informed advice on the state of the arts in the region. (This expertise can be supplemented if necessary by specialists from other parts of the country.) On-the-spot access of this kind would help dispel the air of have-not helplessness that can envelop regions far from the centres of power and—not an insignificant factor—help defuse the often-expressed resentment of those who condemn the federal grant-distribution process as a massive back-scratching network.

The framework of federal regional councils, created to deal with a range of pressing social issues in a horizontal manner, might provide the managerial and policy skills on which to base such a move. Local levels of government must also play an expanded legislative role, particularly by integrating cultural policies into urban planning, and better ways must be found to harmonize cultural policies across the various levels of government. Collaborative networks intersecting with various levels of government could play a significant role in shaping policy.

The Canada Council for the Arts, for its part, should seriously rethink its policies on regional offices and officer travel to the regions (a valuable contact with the field that suffered significantly in the cut-back years). Access to local voices and an attentive understanding of creative developments at city and regional levels will be crucial to the development of positive policies and effective programs. At the same time, decentralization will affirm the Council's commitment to the entire constituency of Canadian creativity.

I O

THE CANADA COUNCIL
FOR THE ARTS

In financial terms—and considering the taxes I've paid on the income
even from this one book alone—the taxpayers' investment in me
through this tiny $7,000 grant is possibly the best investment they
ever made. If I had been a penny stock, I'd be written up in every
financial journal on the planet.

—MARGARET ATWOOD on the grant she received from
the Canada Council for the Arts to write her
1972 book, *Surfacing*

THE CANADA COUNCIL for the Arts, widely regarded as the country's principal agency for arts funding, was established in 1957 as an arm's-length agency of the federal government. Its role is "to foster and promote the study and enjoyment of, and the production of works in, the arts." As it approaches its golden jubilee, the time is appropriate to assess how well it is doing that job and to tackle a number of fundamental dilemmas that threaten its ability to carry out its mandate.

The timing of the Council's creation, only a decade after the end of the Second World War, was fortuitous. The world was still rediscovering its identity and redefining communal experience, and the sustained support that the Canada Council provided in the early decades of its existence played a significant role in the flourishing of all forms of Canadian artistic expression. Through encouraging the emergence of the authentic voices of Canada's artists, at home and abroad, it helped develop a Canadian distinctiveness at a crucial time.

My grants bought time. If I hadn't had the grants I would have had to find some other way of earning a living, and without large chunks of unstructured time you can't be a writer. In 1982 I had four stepchildren and a baby at home, and school hours and nap time were my only resource. My daughter always said that I made her take naps till she was 18.

—JANE URQUHART on the grants she received from the Canada Council for the Arts in the early stages of her career

However, like many government agencies, the Canada Council went through difficult times in Ottawa's era of economic retrenchment in the early 1990s. With its government funding diminishing, it was forced to cut staff by almost a half to ensure that grant budgets were maintained. The continued existence of several core programs was called into question, among them the Canada Council Art Bank, the world's largest collection of contemporary art, which was forced by economic difficulties to stop acquiring art in 1995.

The experience proved a salutary one. The Council used the opportunity to refine all aspects of its operations, from financial management, business planning and corporate governance to the peer adjudication process. The Art Bank was narrowly saved, and by 2001 it was back in the business of acquiring new artwork for rental. And the renewed and redefined agency that emerged in the late 1990s was rewarded with additions to its base funding budget, notably a $75-million-over-three-years increase announced as part of the May 2001 Tomorrow Starts Today package, an initiative that restored federal cultural funding to pre-cutback levels.

The notion of an arm's-length relationship with government has been a cornerstone of Council operations, and it is vigorously defended across the spectrum of the cultural community. Full authority for all decisions (priorities, policies and funding) rests with the Council, not with government. The principle was summed up by Prime Minister Louis St. Laurent when he recommended the creation of the Council to Parliament: "Government," he said, "should support the cultural development of the nation but not control it." This principle provides double insulation: government and politicians are protected from the immediate fallout over controversial funding decisions, and the Council is free to make its decisions without fear of political interference. (The Council operates with the same degree of autonomy as the CBC, the National Arts Centre and Telefilm Canada.)

However, this is not to suggest that the Canada Council should operate in a vacuum. It is an agency of the federal government, and it is in the agency's own best interests—legally, it can be argued that it is its *responsibility*—to remain aware of the broad directions in which the government of the day is moving.

The line here is fine. The Council's independence is jealously guarded, and rightly so. It cannot allow itself to be compromised by carrying out tasks that are overtly political: funnelling funds to a named arts organization in a specific political riding, for instance, or refusing a grant to an individual or a project frowned upon by officialdom. At the same time, the Council's activities encompass more than the mere distribution of grants, and it is possible to find areas of arts development where the Council and various government departments (particularly the Department of Canadian Heritage) have shared interests and where a collaborative approach, cautiously explored, can pay dividends for both.

Profile-raising is one of these areas. Advocacy for the cultural sector is clearly an area where the Council can bring both expertise and connections to the table. Audience development is another area in which strategies can be developed to the benefit of both parties. In its assessment of grants to arts organizations the Council often includes a weighting for audience-building activity, recognizing that the act of making art implies an audience and that developing this audience remains a pressing challenge. The Council has also developed finely focussed programs intended to upgrade the quality of arts management, distribution and presenting—all significant concerns of other areas of government involved in cultural funding.

Fundamental, too, are matters of cultural equity and the support of aboriginal artistic activity, both of high concern to the Department of Canadian Heritage (DOCH). Since 1989, the Council has steadily intensified its efforts to strengthen equity and diversity both within the organization and in its responses to the cultural community. Aboriginal artists from diverse cultures now make up at least 20 per cent of peer assessment panels, and information for first-time applicants is available in French, English, Mandarin, Spanish, Punjabi and Inuktitut.

Despite the significant additions to its base budget in recent years, however, the Council is still badly underfunded, and the Council has identified as a priority the need to demonstrate both to DOCH and to government generally what Council director John Hobday calls "the absolute necessity of a significant increase in the Council's appropriation." More than 15,000 grant applications are received each year; fewer than a third of these are successful, and awards are often for a lesser amount than requested. And despite the Council's popular image as the main fount of Canada's cultural funding, it handles only 4 per cent of federal spending on culture. In 1999–2000, the federal cultural budget totalled $2.8 billion, or $92 per Canadian citizen. Canada Council grants (including payments to authors under the Public Lending Right Commission) totalled $111 million, or $3.58 per Canadian.

This acute shortage of money is at the root of one of the most pernicious, and potentially most destructive, arguments both inside the

Council and in the broader cultural community: the debate about who gets what.

Who Gets What?

BETWEEN THE MID-1990s and the start of the new century, the number of organizations on the Council's books almost doubled, to 1,700. This was largely in response to its 1995 strategic plan, which specified that greater access should be provided to previously under-represented areas of the cultural community, among them aboriginal and culturally diverse artists and arts organizations, and interdisciplinary artists. These organizations, along with organizations providing programming for young audiences, made up most of the incoming numbers. (The phenomenon is not limited to the Canada Council: provincial arts agencies are seeing similar growth in their clientele.)

The Council's increases in its funding in recent years have been substantial, but they have not kept pace with the growth in eligible applicants, which has put intense pressure on its resources. Increasingly, it is not a matter of being good or not: people cannot even get through the door. There simply is not enough money to do the job, and in that sense, the Canada Council is the author of its own misfortunes. In the first forty-plus years of its existence, it has carried out its responsibility to foster the arts so well, and so effectively, that it has created a monster it is unable to feed.

One area of fierce discussion involves the funding of Canada's large-scale performing-arts organizations. Repeated studies and a mountain of paper evidence show that our major organizations are significantly underfunded. Orchestras teeter routinely on the brink of ruin. Ballet companies are forced to trim their economic cloth to the detriment of what they put on the stage.

The June 2001 study of large performing-arts organizations conducted for the Council showed that our biggest and brightest are in dire need of substantial new money if they are to fulfil their potential and answer audience needs in the years ahead—far more money, in fact, than the Council is able to provide. Even if the Council's grants budget was devoted in its entirety to these organizations, this would be no more than a stop-gap. Our biggest orchestras, opera companies, theatre companies and ballet troupes have become major businesses in their own right. Yet—such is the nature of the artistic enterprise—they can have no reasonable hope of survival, and certainly no hope of growth, without significant help from the public purse.

Solid arguments exist for the underwriting of our major arts organizations to a far greater degree than is currently the case. These organizations keep us rooted in an awareness of our cultural origins as well as providing yardsticks of excellence in contemporary perform-ance. They contribute significantly to the country's cultural identity, they carry our image proudly abroad, they give work and experience to our performing artists, they help sustain the cultural life of their communities: without the work they provide, talented artists and teachers might well be forced to go elsewhere.

Playwright Michael Healey, interviewed in *Saturday Night* in May 2002, gave eloquent voice to the effect of financial restraint on perhaps the most important issue of all, the sustenance of creative excellence and daring. In his view, the quality of work at the Stratford Festival has declined as the demand to generate new revenue streams to replace disappearing government subsidies has intensified. Sometimes while watching a show at Stratford, he said, "My mind will drift and I'll fan-tasize about a place that doesn't talk proudly about how less than five per cent of its budget comes from subsidy. A place that gets a third of its revenue (like England's Royal Shakespeare Company) from tax dol-lars; a place that, because of this, has been freed to experiment with the classics while seriously developing new work. And when the lights come up ... I realize that it's not a new Stratford I was dreaming about.

I was fantasizing about living in a country that recognizes the value of a place like the Stratford Festival."

However, the dilemma the Council faces is a cruel one. Should it devote itself to shoring up the majors, in the hope that they will keep the entire enterprise afloat—the "few but roses" scenario of its early days? If it does that, what will happen to the mid-range and emerging companies, the small-town galleries, the multitude of individual artists who rely on the Council both for validation and for sustenance? A Canada Council grant of $2 million may be small change to Stratford, but it is a substantial chunk of the Council's overall theatre budget—which must also try to deal equitably with all the other excellent theatre creators and producers who clamour for attention.

Should the Council get ruthless with organizations that cannot keep their overdrafts under control, cutting off anyone whose accumulated deficits reach a certain proportion of their operating budget? (Under the current system, the principle seems to be the bigger the financial hole, the larger the bailout.)

Should the Council set an upper limit on the size of its subventions? Currently, large organizations consume what looks like a disproportionate amount of the available funding, leaving smaller organizations and individuals comparative crumbs. To take just one example, the National Ballet of Canada's annual grant of around $2 million, while widely regarded as insufficient, represents about 15 per cent of the dance section's annual budget.

Should the Council reconsider the priorities against which it measures its applicants? If, for instance, evaluations were weighted more heavily than they are at present for factors such as youth, community outreach, aboriginals, minority cultures, arts education—all of which are high priorities for both the Council and the government—the distribution of funds would probably be very different from the way it stands now.

Should it wave goodbye to the big organizations altogether, particularly those running surpluses: send them off, like graduates leaving home after a long period of nurturing, to make their own way in the big wide world? Alternatively, should it ask the government to establish a separate fund, perhaps within the Council, devoted entirely to the major arts organizations, as defined by budget size?

From time to time, it has even been suggested that support for individual artists or emerging companies be curtailed so the major companies can be funded appropriately. This proposal usually surfaces at times of dire crisis, when this or that jewel in our cultural crown is apparently about to roll down history's drain. Administering many often-minuscule individual grants (they amount to about 20 per cent of the Council's annual grants budget overall) is a lengthy and expensive process, with a disproportionate workload attached. In addition, these small grants rarely deliver "profile" for the Council and, as R&D investments, offer no guarantee of product delivery.

The two sides of this argument will never be reconciled. Of course we need our major organizations. Equally, though, we have an obligation to nurture our emerging artists. Individual creativity is the bedrock of everything the Council exists for. It is here that we test ideas, attitudes and approaches, not all of which could survive in the open market. (In the same way, we support the public broadcaster in its provision of programming that offers an alternative to that provided by commercial concerns.) Individual grants are the basis on which many artists—from all disciplines, from all Canada's cultures—can get a jump-start on their careers. These grants provide a necessary incubation period in which young artists can develop their individuality and professional skills. They keep the Council in touch with the emerging artistic community, allowing it to respond with flexibility to new styles and movements. They give artists in mid-career an opportunity to take stock. They provide sustenance for senior artists who would not otherwise be able to survive in the marketplace. They are, in other words, fuel to the entire creative process.

Singer Wendy Nielsen, from Cambridge Narrows, New Brunswick, received a Career Development Grant from the Canada Council for the Arts in 1995. A second grant helped her travel to New York for an audition with the New York Philharmonic Orchestra, where she won bookings to perform in Penderecki's Seven Gates of Jerusalem *and other presentations. She has subsequently performed throughout Canada and Europe. "The Career Development Grant had a tremendous impact on my career," she says, "and for this I am forever grateful."*

A consultant's study in 1999 made it clear that Canada Council grants give individuals "artistic freedom" and have a profound effect on their creative lives and careers. Nonetheless, the Council has long admitted that it cannot keep up with the growth of the individual artist community in Canada. In 1998–99, $18.3 million was awarded to individual artists and creators out of a total budget of $98.7 million. Any proposal to reduce individual support would be reminiscent of the argument for arts organization "birth control" advanced by some Council thinkers in the 1970s. Intervention of this kind—the French term, *dirigisme,* is perhaps more accurate—has no place in the policies of an agency with the responsibilities of the Canada Council.

Rather than withdrawing from this area of support, the Canada Council should mount a lobbying campaign to augment funds to support individual artists. Serious consideration should be given to the reinstitution of the Explorations program, or something like it, setting aside dedicated funding for younger and emerging artists across disciplines and cultures. This would restore the adventure and interdisciplinary openness so fundamental to the success of Explorations, a program abandoned at a time of budgetary restraint and replaced by separate programs of individual artist support within the various disciplines. For the ongoing health of Canadian culture, we cannot allow ourselves to eat our young.

Another dilemma the Council must sooner or later deal with (though it shows no relish for the task) is the way it slices its budgetary pie among the various disciplines. Each of the six sections within the Arts Division (music, theatre, dance, visual arts, writing and publishing, and media arts) is allocated a budgetary amount for its annual activities. Although the amounts for each discipline fluctuate according to the base amount available for any particular year, the proportion on which they are distributed has remained roughly the same for decades. (Media and interdisciplinary arts have forced their way onto the table in a modest way in recent years.) No one is able to pin down how the original proportions were arrived at (the persuasive powers of early officers seem to have had a lot to do with it), and no one seems willing to open up the envelopes. But that is precisely what common sense says should be done. The arts are always in process. New weightings occur; emerging art forms demand attention; whole disciplines can take on new authority and importance.

It is time, in fact, for a wholesale re-examination of the parameters within which the Council works. These big questions have been danced around for long enough. It is time for the Council to pull them together in a public forum: a conference, not another consultation, and public for reasons I will clarify in a moment.

At this conference, the Council's officers should be invited to support their bids for more cash with all the arguments they can muster. Experts from all sides should be heard: arts administrators, representatives from various cultures, futurists. The people who hold the government purse strings should be brought in to listen and watch.

All the big issues should be on the table. Arguments should be heard, pro and con, for preferential support for individual artists, bailouts for the big twenty-nine, new emphasis on aboriginal arts, arts in the community and artists in the schools. Tears will be shed, hair will be torn, garments will be rent.

Holding this gathering in public would signal recognition that Canada and the Canadian cultural community are at a nexus of momentous change—change that will influence what the Council does and how effectively it supports its growing and changing community. And after the last statistical chart has been flashed across the screen, after the last dancer/actor/writer has pleaded the cause, after the last inspirational aria has illuminated the discourse, a team made up of senior Council staff—but not predominantly senior Council staff—and thoughtful, generous-minded leaders from the cultural community (of which there are many) should synthesize the findings into an action plan.

The plan might not prove so different from those the Council has had all along. But the process would demonstrate that wisdom in these matters is not exclusive to the Council. That act alone would do wonders for advocacy of the arts. And as a gesture of inclusiveness, it would reinforce the Council's belief in the importance of the views of the community it is there to serve.

Who Decides?

"NOTHING," SAID THE POET Philip Larkin, "is harder to form than an estimate even remotely accurate of our own contemporary artists." No one is more aware of the truth of Larkin's statement than the management and board members of the Canada Council. Many individual grants distributed by the Council fall into the category of "risk money"—that is, they are speculations on potential delivery. Even grants to publishers, galleries and orchestras carry no guarantee. The Council must identify, to the best of its ability, that which has the most potential to deliver excellence.

Who should decide that? The Council has evolved over the years a system of peer assessment as the basis for its grant-making decisions. Applications from individuals, projects and organizations are adjudicated by panels of professionals from the field, chosen for their credibility, expertise, knowledge of the community, fair-mindedness and experience. The panels are balanced, to the extent that such balance is possible in a group of (typically) five individuals, for geography, gender, language, range of artistic practice, age and cultural diversity. An attempt is made, in other words, to mirror the Canadian reality on these panels, in order that grants be distributed as equitably as possible.

The system is not, by any means, exclusive to the Council. Many other funding bodies in the humanities, the sciences and the professions, as well as prize juries such as the Nobel and Pulitzer, use a similar process. Like most systems of its kind, it is open to abuse, and a certain amount of cynicism and mistrust is felt outside the Council. The arguments against peer panels have to do with perceptions that they are closed systems of cliques rewarding cliques and because of that do not reflect general tastes and values. Officers are sometimes suspected of rigging panel membership to obtain a particular result.

The Council staff and board have tinkered extensively with the details in an effort to ensure fairness, and what has resulted is generally (though not universally) considered the best available process in the circumstances. For all the cynicism, it says much for the integrity and transparency of the process, and the regard in which it is held, that the decisions the Council's juries make are rarely challenged, and then usually by individuals outside the arts community who wish to express their outrage over what they perceive as misguided use of public funds.

Several hundred individuals are on the Council's active list of potential jurors at any one time, and in a year approximately 500 are invited to participate on about 120 committees. Their work is augmented by about 200 independent assessors who submit reports on specific performances or other artworks. As a rule, an individual can be a member of an assessment panel only once every two years, and grant recipients must wait two years from the date of their own award before being able to take part.

One of the spinoff benefits of the process is that it lets professionals in the field mix with and learn from other experts while being exposed to a sampling of the best the field has to offer. In addition, knowing that their work will be given a serious look by people they respect, grant applicants are encouraged to find ways to articulate what they do and why they do it.

Although the Canada Council has used juries of peers almost since its inception, pressure has from time to time been felt to incorporate non-specialist individuals into the decision-making mix. The Ontario Arts Council, for example, has experimented with broadening grant adjudication panels to include knowledgeable volunteers from the arts field, alongside the standard mix of artists, administrators and other professionals.

The question of how much involvement the community should have in the spending of public money is a contentious one. Certainly, government funding comes with certain requirements attached. Prime among these are accountability, transparency and effectiveness. The arguments for including non-specialists in the decision-making process are essentially, perhaps even aggressively, anti-elitist in nature, often presented as a matter of giving the taxpayers who support the arts a chance to decide what is supported (though no one ever suggests amateur enthusiasts should make decisions on how we spend tax dollars on armaments or medical research).

The danger here is that a jury of this kind would be less likely to identify and endorse the edgy, the unexpected: less likely to create a climate in which the seeds of anarchy and disturbance—freshness of thought, really—could grow. Even among a group of experienced professional artists, the temptation exists to confer validation on the known and to stick with the reasonably predictable. Introducing what some artists call civilians to the mix would in all likelihood only blunt the keenness to explore new frontiers.

The process of awarding operating grants to arts organizations is somewhat more complicated. Hobday is uncompromising on the issue of excellence. The Canada Council, he says, will fund only artists and organizations that maintain "high standards of excellence in accordance with our competition criteria. We will be forgiving of bad luck," he says. "We will be forgiving of occasional failure when it is balanced by successes. But the overall criterion of excellence will be firmly enforced." However, assessments of artistic merit and professional excellence are augmented by other criteria: community connections, outreach, audience development, and issues such as managerial and financial stability. Historical precedent also plays a part (in the United States, on the other hand, grants in the arts are almost entirely project based). In Canada, arts organizations develop a history of funding from the Council, and their grants tend to be tied to that. Amounts might increase or decrease according to the achievements of any particular year, and occasionally organizations that consistently fail to make the grade might be cut off entirely, but in most cases a certain anticipation of support becomes established.

Increasing numbers of organizations are "multi-year" grant recipients—that is, they are given guarantees that they will receive grants of a certain amount for a two- or three-year period, so long as their record of artistic achievement is maintained. The benefits of this sustained help are obvious: more opportunity for long-term planning, more stable employment for staff and artists, more room to breathe, the assurance of an extended period of time to do what they are there for—make art. For artists, this gift of time is the greatest gift that society can provide. However, when funds are finite—and far short of demand—companies with a history of success can, simply by the bulk of their presence, keep newer companies outside the door. Canada

Council officers routinely plead that they are unable to do justice to the number of deserving candidates in their annual competitions. More money to the Canada Council for the Arts will enable it to place more organizations—not only the big, predictable names, but mid- to small-size companies—under this security blanket.

At the same time, the Council must keep a rigorous watch on the level of achievement of this privileged group of beneficiaries. Arts organizations, like other organisms, go through cycles of life; the Council must be prepared to let them go if they lose their edge. There is no such thing as automatic entitlement, whatever some arts administrators may wish to believe; the competition for available funds is too intense for that.

This raises another question, again related to juries and assessment. As the diversity and number of individuals and organizations continues to grow, how does the Council cleave to the principle of artistic excellence, a central pillar in all it does, and at the same time continue to democratize? How does it ensure that the criterion of merit is fairly applied? As new forms of art emerge and as fresh cultural traditions enter the Council's embrace, definitions of excellence come under fresh scrutiny. It is therefore doubly important that the Council and its officers ensure that juries and assessors are as informed about their discipline as possible.

It is tempting to suggest that some form of preferential, catch-up support should be given to emerging art forms and cultural communities. However, this argument should not beguile us into any lessening of expectations. The doors to possibility must remain open, and keeping them open is part of the responsibility of our cultural development agencies, particularly the Canada Council. But the danger with this democracy and pluralism is that the idea of excellence will inevitably take a beating. When everything is given equal significance, how do we distinguish works of genuine merit from the mediocre?

Sooner or later, tests must be applied. The solution is not to lower expectations, but to ensure that the expertise in decision-making recruited at all levels is properly representative.

Aboriginal Arts

THE FIRST YEAR THE Canada Council for the Arts funded aboriginal artists was 1969; four applied and two were given grants. The number of applications increased slowly: 165 between 1969 and 1982, just under 1,000 in the next dozen years, and about double that between 1996 and 1999, by which time the grant level in all disciplines had reached $2.3 million a year. The increase to the Canada Council's budget from the Tomorrow Starts Today fund in 2001 enabled the Council to add $800,000 to the amounts granted each year to aboriginal artists and organizations, for a total of about $4.4 million in 2001–02.

Zacharias Kunuk would never have been able to make his award-winning film Atanarjuat *(The Fast Runner), set in the High Arctic, on an Inuit theme and in subtitled Inuktituk, without the support of public money. The Canada Council for the Arts, the National Film Board and Telefilm Canada all contributed at various stages in the creative process to its $2-million budget. In an era when Canadian movie success is generally measured by star-vehicle hits like* Men with Brooms, Atanarjuat *has become one of Canada's most successful films. And while that crucial support enabled Kunuk to bring his project to fruition, it also—perhaps even more importantly—put the movie world on notice: that Canada's native peoples are a creative force to be reckoned with, and that a movie made in one of Canada's "ancestral languages" can be both an artistic and a box-office success.*

The Council's Aboriginal Arts Secretariat, established in 1994, ensures that Council-wide policies, budgets, grant programs and program infrastructure include and promote aboriginal artists. It coordinates aboriginal representation on the advisory groups and peer assessment juries consulted by the officers of the various disciplines; administers the Aboriginal Peoples Collaborative Exchange, which encourages collaborative projects and dialogue on innovation and tradition; and keeps watch over grants programming to ensure that aboriginal needs are met. In addition, each of the six arts disciplines has an aboriginal program officer, and each discipline has evolved its own network of programs targeted at aboriginal artists.

In recent years, insistent pressure has been brought to bear on the Council, through its aboriginal advisory committee, to replace the current structure with a stand-alone Aboriginal Arts Office. This would take over the aboriginal programs that currently exist within the various disciplines, centralize aboriginal funding within the Council, have the same ranking as the Arts Division (which looks after all the disciplines), and report directly to the Council's director—effectively, it would create independence for aboriginal arts within the Council, complete with designated funding and a full staff.

The arguments for an Aboriginal Arts Office rest on the assertion that the cultural traditions of the original peoples of Canada deserve special status within the Council, that the federal government has a responsibility to provide that recognition and protection, that aboriginal cultural traditions are not understood or recognized by the mainstream and have largely been excluded from the structures of national cultural institutions, and that despite the efforts of the Canada Council to redress these inequities, the needs of aboriginal artists are still not being adequately met.

However, these arguments seem to plead for a kind of affirmative action that would ghettoize aboriginal arts at precisely the time when such a separation is least needed—a time of unprecedented interconnectedness across disciplines and cultures. To separate aboriginal funding programs from the programs that serve the rest of Canada's artists would only perpetuate the sense of difference and otherness that we should, as a society, be at pains to eliminate.

The Council's communications section must intensify its outreach efforts to ensure that aboriginal artists throughout Canada are aware of the availability of Council funding for their work, and the application process should be tailored to the needs of the various communities it serves. Continuing efforts must be also made to sensitize all Council staff to the issues surrounding aboriginal arts representation and funding.

Most importantly, the Council should ensure that sufficient programs are developed in every arts discipline to make it possible for aboriginal artists and arts organizations to fulfil their potential in the face of specific challenges. In the case of theatre groups, for instance, the aboriginal community has highlighted a number of problems, among them the lack of a pool of experienced talent for companies to draw on, their relative geographic isolation, and their need for professional development aid and better access to the Council's theatre funding programs. These problems cannot be solved with a quick fix; they must be addressed over the long term. As one aboriginal observer put it: "To address the historical inequities takes serious, ongoing commitment. When we look at how long it took to build mainstream [white] theatre companies and the years of funding that they received, five years, or even ten years, is a mere flash in the pan in comparison."

What must also be recognized and accommodated is the fact that aboriginal creativity draws on diverse principles that embody both traditional knowledge and contemporary arts practice. An issue that has relevance to this discussion is the tension between ideas of individuality (the importance of which tends to be at the basis of mainstream artistic creativity) and communality (that is, ceremony and ritual, an integral function of some traditional aboriginal art). For the purposes of grant adjudication, how do you compare, for example, ballet and powwow dancing? How do you separate art designed for performance from art made primarily for ceremonial purposes? The challenge is to find equitable means to evaluate—and support—the creative activity of all Canadian artists.

It is a highly complex and politically loaded issue, not just for Canadian aboriginal art but for the art forms of many of Canada's diverse and minority cultures, and for every other agency that funds aboriginal creativity (the Department of Canadian Heritage, for instance). It is also an issue that demands a great investment of trust and goodwill from both sides. As Ashok Mathur put it in his introduction to "Race Poetry, Eh?", a special edition of the Winnipeg-based literary magazine *Prairie Fire* to mark World Poetry Day and the International Day for the Elimination of Racial Discrimination in 2001: "As much as we might like to believe in the good will of those around us and those who govern us, there are other, more complicated forces at work that we often choose not to see."

He was referring specifically to a UN committee's condemnation in 1998 of Canada's lack of progress in alleviating social and economic hardship among aboriginals and its concern about "the direct connection between Aboriginal economic marginalization and the ongoing dispossession of Aboriginal people from their lands." However, Mathur said, "I do not wish to dismiss those good intentions as mere façades"—and it is that implicit goodwill, on both sides of the debate, on which we must build if we are to reach a just and lasting resolution.

Arts Education: The Role of the Council

THE CANADA COUNCIL RECENTLY renewed its commitment to youth and the development of young audiences, recognizing that its responsibilities in this area go beyond the specific needs of the organizations and individuals it supports. It is time now for the Council to be given the resources that will allow it to significantly increase its attention to arts education in every meaning of the term: that is, education *in* the arts, education *through* the arts and education *for* the arts.

Enabling artists and arts organizations to make contact with young audiences is a continuing concern. Among the next steps the Council could take might be the following:

- Give renewed high priority to support for individual and organizational creation, production and dissemination of work for young audiences across the full extent of Council programs.
- Make grants available to teachers who wish to improve their arts expertise and to artists who wish to improve their skills in the classroom.
- Facilitate innovative collaborations between artists/arts organizations and educators.
- Establish working partnerships with other national and provincial arts organizations (orchestras, theatre companies, museums, galleries, the new Virtual Museum of Canada and agencies such as the Canadian Conference of the Arts), both to build networks of advice and action and to create new forms of access for young audiences.
- Aggressively pursue links with the Council of Ministers of Education, Canada, with the aim of establishing a climate of opinion that would lead to the integration of arts education within the general curriculum.
- Facilitate interdisciplinary arts-science crossover studies in schools, taught by Council-funded artists.
- Consider involving outside expertise for third-party delivery of these services, under the Council umbrella.

To ensure the continued thriving of Canadian creativity, we also need to nurture our developing artistic community—those who are emerging, and those who are yet to come. That means serious attention to training as well as money to let young artists test themselves and experiment.

However, training for the arts community has been a contentious issue for the Canada Council. During the cutback years of the 1990s, support for national training organizations was discontinued, in part on the grounds that the Council did not have the expertise to assess these programs effectively, and in part because they did not fit the Council's overall mandate.

This is clearly no longer the case, if it ever was. As proposed in the next section, the Council should re-examine its responsibility for funding arts training, with a particular view to supporting training organizations in the performing arts—including training in non-European traditions.

Canada Council for the Arts: Catalyst for Growth

LEAN, TRANSPARENT, ACCOUNTABLE and flexible in its thinking, economical in the delivery of its programs, and able to make its decisions an important arm's length away from government, the Canada Council for the Arts has developed a wide-ranging, nuanced portfolio of policies to carry out its mission of fostering Canadian cultural creativity and making it accessible to Canadians.

Persuasive arguments can now be made for giving the Council a strengthened leadership role in turning future-oriented policies of access, excellence and financial stability into reality. As a beginning, the Council's appropriation should be materially increased. The Council has received generous increases in its annual allotment from government in the years since the cutback era of the 1990s. However, given the effects of inflation, the growth of Canada's population and the increasing demands of Canada's aboriginal and culturally diverse communities, much more is needed. Let us suggest the appropriation

($127.4 million in the 2000–01 year) is doubled—for convenience, to $250 million. Promises of future increases would be tied to the tangible demonstration of the success of its programs in such areas as growth in audiences, greater integration of cultural activity into the community, and greater involvement of aboriginals and diverse cultures in both arts creation and participation—all of which can be easily measured year to year.

It is important to explore this proposal for increased responsibility cautiously. The Council's arm's-length independence must be jealously guarded. And as we have seen, it is not always possible to demonstrate an immediate payoff from investment in creativity, particularly where individuals are concerned. All arts grants are risks. However, the Canada Council has more than four decades of experience in placing informed money on likely prospects. Its peer evaluation system, while undergoing constant scrutiny and frequent refinement, is widely regarded as the best and fairest available. Its track record in developing Canadian creativity in the arts is unparalleled. And its expertise in managing cultural funds in a transparent, economical manner, honed to a fine sharpness during the "program review" years, is well established.

The Council's activities encompass far more than the distribution of grants, and many areas exist in which the Council and various government departments already exercise a limited form of collaboration. It might now be time to integrate at least some of these programs under the Council umbrella, and the Council board is already in discussion with DOCH about what Hobday discreetly calls "a redistribution of responsibilities between the Council and the department." Non-Council programs for such things as festivals, arts presenting, foreign touring, community cultural development, and arts education and training are obvious candidates for transfer of this kind.

Advocacy and profile-raising are areas in which the Council has experience and expertise. It has many success stories to tell, and its mission to spread the word to all corners of Canada about the public funds available for cultural activity dovetails with the interests of other government departments. Audience development and many aspects of arts management are other areas of shared concern.

The research and development aspect of creative activity is another area in which Council activities overlap with the interests of other agencies, as is the need to ensure that Canada's artists are able to take advantage of the expressive potential of the new technology. Fundamental, too, are the issues of representing Canada's artistic achievements to the wider world, cultural equity, the support of aboriginal artistic activity, and the upgrading of arts management.

Yet another challenge is broadening the base of cultural activity within Canada's communities. The Council shares with other cultural agencies the obligation to build bridges between the cultural community and both the private sector and the community at large, and to build partnerships with other organizations, such as libraries, broadcasters and universities. This is already done to a degree through residencies, commissions, performance opportunities, prizes, awards and other forms of recognition that both "employ" the artist and expose new audiences to the arts. But many community-based arts programs—programs that for many young individuals provide the key first contact with art and art-making—currently have difficulty getting federal funding. Given the Council's commitment to art in the community, this is another area in which the Council, in collaboration with other agencies, could take a primary role.

A transfer of responsibilities and resources of this magnitude would inevitably provoke fresh thinking and new policies and programs from the Council's board and management. Most importantly, in what it would demonstrate about political commitment to the development of Canada's cultural identity, it could well expose the lie in the politician's regretful assertion that there's no vote in culture.

E N V O I

There is one thing stronger than all the armies of the world,
and that is an idea whose time has come.

—VICTOR HUGO

I DEALISTIC, ALL THIS? Yes, but pragmatically idealistic. The pressures of the day-to-day in our market-based society are daunting; we hope for long-term vision but settle for fleeting opportunism. To maintain a distinctive, pluralistic Canada in which its people's stories are heard and valued, we must nourish the elements that manifest that uniqueness. It is a task the cultural community and government must approach together, with the generous and undisguised intent of making this great public wealth freely available. Daunting, yes. But it can be done. All that is necessary is the will.

The ultimate measure of how closely we approach this ideal will be the extent to which Canadians embrace creation, innovation and difference as an integral part of their lives. If we deeply believe, in our beings, that culture and the arts transcend the everyday; if we know in our hearts that books and plays and dances and music and films and paintings and sculptures are vessels in which we can discover the limitless pleasures and fascinations of this mysterious life we share; if we recognize in our souls that it is in intuition and imagination that we find ways to connect with the enduring human truths; if we agree that the norm must be challenged to uncover alternatives worth pursuing; if we recognize that "to re-enchant our lives in a disenchanted culture" (to use the words of Thomas Moore) we must reforge the vital link between the artist and the people, then it becomes a simple matter.

When each of us adds our individual weight to the groundswell of persuasion, soon enough we create an unstoppable force, and our world becomes a better, more humane place, where questions can be asked without fear, differences can be celebrated without rancour, and the thrilling diversity of human expression can be freely shared by all Canadians.

A C K N O W L E D G E M E N T S

F OR HELP IN PREPARING this book I have many people to thank. The project was originally proposed to me by the former deputy minister of the Department of Canadian Heritage, Alex Himelfarb, subsequently clerk of the Privy Council and an ardent believer in the need to articulate arguments in support of Canada's cultural sector. His encouragement and insights were invaluable, as was the advice of many of his colleagues at the department, particularly Hubert Lussier and Cynthia White-Thornley, as well as Ted Bairstow, Linda Johnston, Elizabeth McKinnon, Roma Quapp, Tamara Feick, Glen Mostowich and Bruno Jean. Many individuals in Canada's cultural community have generously shared their views and visions, particularly

John Hobday, Jocelyn Harvey, Peter Herrndorf, Scott McIntyre and my valued former board colleagues at the Canada Council for the Arts, principal among them Jean-Louis Roux, François Colbert, Dean Brinton, Riki Turofsky, Suzanne Rochon Burnett, Nalini Stewart, Jeannita Thériault, John McKellar and the late Carol Shields. Council staff, both past and present, whose ongoing assistance and insights have been helpful include Shirley L. Thomson, John Goldsmith, Lisa Roberts, Gordon Platt, Anne Valois, Micheline Lesage, Keith Kelly, Sharon Fernandez, André Courchesne, Claude Schryer, Barbara Benoit, Claire McCaughey and Donna Balkan. I have been particularly fortunate to have input and commentary from a broad range of other interested individuals, among them Milton Wong, Margaret Somerville, Katherine Berg, David Walden, Megan Williams, Burke Taylor, Duncan Low, Margaret Reynolds, Barbara Clausen, Robert Sunter, Brian Fawcett, Timothy Porteous, the late Jean-Pierre Perreault, Paul-André Fortier, Cathy Levy, Robert Palmer, Norman Armour, Wendy Newman, Ron Burnett and my insightful editors at Douglas & McIntyre, Barbara Pulling and Naomi Pauls.

None of it would have been possible, however, without the constant support and candid commentary of my wife, Susan Mertens. Despite debilitating illness, her belief in the value of what the book has to say and her insistence that it be said with force and clarity never flagged.

BIBLIOGRAPHY

Books

Appleyard, Bryan. *The Culture Club: Crisis in the Arts*. London: Faber & Faber, 1984.

———. *Brave New Worlds: Staying Human in the Genetic Future*. Toronto: Viking, 1998.

Battiste, Marie, and James (Sa'ke'j) Youngblood Henderson. *Protecting Indigenous Knowledge and Heritage: A Global Challenge*. Saskatoon: Purich Publishing, 2000.

Benedict, Stephen. *Public Money and the Muse: Essays on Government Funding for the Arts*. New York: W. W. Norton, 1991.

Blaser, Robin, and Robert Dunham, eds. *Art and Reality: A Casebook of Concern*. Conference proceedings, Simon Fraser University. Vancouver: Talonbooks, 1986.

Byatt, A.S. Preface to *Strange and Charmed: Science and the Contemporary Visual Arts*. London: Gulbenkian Foundation, 2000.

Cameron, Silver Donald. *The ArtSmarts Story*. Canadian Conference of the Arts, 2000.

Carruthers, Glen, and Gordana Lazarevich. *A Celebration of Canada's Arts, 1930–1970.* Toronto: Canadian Scholars Press, 1996.

Colbert, François, ed. *Cultural Organizations of the Future.* Colloquium proceedings, Ecole des Hautes Etudes Commerciales, Montreal, 1997.

Downey, James, and Lois Claxton. *Inno'va-tion: Essays by Leading Canadian Researchers.* Toronto: Key Porter, 2002.

Florida, Richard. *The Rise of the Creative Class: And How It's Transforming Work, Leisure, Community and Everyday Life.* New York: Basic Books, 2002.

Friedman, Thomas L. *The Lexus and the Olive Tree.* New York: Farrar, Straus & Giroux, 2000.

Gladwell, Malcolm. *The Tipping Point: How Little Things Can Make a Big Difference.* Boston: Little Brown, 2000.

Hall, Peter. *Cities in Civilization: Culture, Innovation and Urban Order.* London: Weidenfeld & Nicolson, 1998.

Henighan, Tom. *The Presumption of Culture: Structure, Strategy and Survival in the Canadian Cultural Landscape.* Vancouver: Raincoast, 1996.

————. *Ideas of North: A Guide to Canadian Arts and Culture.* Vancouver: Raincoast, 1997.

Homer-Dixon, Thomas. *The Ingenuity Gap: Can We Solve the Problems of the Future?* Toronto: Vintage Canada, 2001.

Hughes, Robert. *Culture of Complaint: The Fraying of America.* New York: Oxford University Press, 1993.

Kramer, Hilton, and Roger Kimball, eds. *Against the Grain: The New Criterion on Art and Intellect at the End of the Twentieth Century.* Chicago: Ivan R. Dee, 1995.

Lasch, Christopher. *The Revolt of the Elites and the Betrayal of Democracy.* New York: W. W. Norton, 1995.

Leadbeater, Charles. *Living on Thin Air: The New Economy.* New York: Viking, 1999.

Mayor, Federico, and Jérôme Bindé. *The World Ahead: Our Future in the Making.* Paris/London: UNESCO/Zed Books, 2001.

Moyers, Bill D. *The Language of Life: A Festival of Poets.* New York: Bantam Doubleday Dell, 1995.

Pettigrew, Pierre S. *The New Politics of Confidence.* Toronto: Stoddart, 1999.

Putnam, Robert D. *Bowling Alone: The Collapse and Revival of American Community.* New York: Simon & Schuster, 2000.

Saul, John Ralston. *Reflections of a Siamese Twin: Canada at the End of the Twentieth Century.* Toronto: Viking, 1997.

Schafer, D. Paul. *Canadian Culture: Key to Canada's Future Development.* Markham, ON: World Cutlure Project, 1995.

Schiller, Herbert L. *The Corporate Takeover of Public Expression.* New York: Oxford University Press, 1989.

Smith, Chris. *Creative Britain.* London: Faber & Faber, 1998.

Tusa, John. *Art Matters: Reflecting on Culture.* London: Methuen, 1999.

Winterson, Jeanette. *Art Objects.* Toronto: Vintage Canada, 1995.

Woodcock, George. *Strange Bedfellows: The State and the Arts in Canada.* Vancouver/ Toronto: Douglas & McIntyre, 1985.

Papers, Speeches and Reports

Annis, Susan. *Arts Education in Canada 2001: An Idea Whose Time Has Come.* Report for the Canada Council for the Arts, March 2001, and supplementary document by Marjorie MacLean, October 2001.

Arts and Heritage Participation Survey. Prepared for the Department of Canadian Heritage by Environics Research Group Limited, September 2000.

Arts Impact Study: Qualitative Summary. Prepared for the Department of Canadian Heritage by Ipsos-Reid, 2002.

Azmier, Jason J. *Culture and Economic Competitiveness: An Emerging Role for the Arts in Canada.* Discussion paper for Canada West Foundation, March 2002.

Burton, Alexandre. "Audio Art Practices." Unpublished paper for the Canada Council for the Arts, April 2001.

Canada's Large Performing Arts Organizations: Improving Conditions for Their Vitality and Sustainability. Report of the Working Group on Large Performing Arts Organizations for the Canada Council for the Arts, June 2001.

Daniel, Sir John. "Technology Is the Answer, But What Is the Question?" Discussion paper for Contact North/Contact Nord, Sudbury, ON, January 2002.

Florida, Richard. *Competing in the Age of Talent: Quality of Place and the New Economy.* Report for the R.K. Mellon Foundation, Heinz Endowments and Sustainable Pittsburgh, January 2000.

———. *The Geography of Bohemia.* January 2001. http://www.heinz.cmu.edu/ ~florida/pages/pub/working_papers/geography.pdf.

Florida, Richard, and Gary Gates. *Technology and Tolerance: The Importance of Diversity to High-Technology Growth.* Center on Urban and Metropolitan Policy, the Brookings Institution, June 2001.

Gertler, Meric, and Richard Florida. *Competing on Creativity: Placing Ontario's Cities in North American Context.* Institute for Competitiveness and Prosperity and Ontario's Ministry of Enterprise, Opportunity and Innovation, 2002.

Harvey, Jocelyn. *Arts in Transition Project:Toward a Culture of Shared Resources.* Canadian Conference of the Arts, October 1977.

————. *Creative Management in the Arts and Heritage: Sustaining and Renewing Professional Management for the 21st Century.* Canadian Conference of the Arts/Cultural Human Resources Council, July 2002. And supplement *Proposed Action Plan for Creating Winning Conditions,* May 2003.

————. *Reflective Space: Report on the Ontario Arts Council's Forum for Arts Specialists and Mentors.* Ontario Arts Council, 2003.

Herrndorf, Peter A. *Bringing Research and Development to Canada's Performing Arts.* National Arts Centre, Ottawa, November 27, 2002.

Hobday, John. Notes for remarks at the Chalmers Conference. Canada Council for the Arts, Ottawa, May 22, 2003.

Jermyn, Helen. *The Arts and Social Exclusion.* A review prepared for the Arts Council of England, 2001.

Kearns, Lendre, and Judy Harquail. *Marketing and Audience Development Practices of Canada's New Music Organizations.* Report for the Canada Council for the Arts, February 2001.

Kushner, Tony. Opening presentation, Grantmakers in the Arts conference, Eureka, CA, October 9, 1995.

A Legacy of Leadership. National Endowment for the Arts, Washington, DC, 2000.

Lewis, Tom, Greg Baeker, and Jane Marsland. *Leadership Development and Renewal: A Learning Strategy for Senior Performing Arts Managers.* Cultural Careers Council Ontario, September 2000.

Monahan, Patrick J. *Culture and the Canadian Constitution.* Common Agenda Alliance for the Arts, Toronto, 1993.

National Symposium on Arts Education. *Sharing the Vision: A National Framework for Arts Education in Canadian Schools.* NASE, 2001.

————. *Making the Vision Happen: A National Framework for Arts Education in Canadian Schools.* NASE, 2002.

Nyvlt, Monica. *Mapping an Artistic Space: Arts Education in Canada (2003).* Canadian Commission for UNESCO, 2003.

Pérez de Cuéllar, Javier. *Our Creative Diversity: Report of the World Commission on Culture and Development.* Paris: UNESCO, 1996.

Piper, Martha C. "Building a Civil Society: A New Role for the Human Sciences." Killam Annual Lecture, Toronto, October 24, 2002.

Restoring the Vision, 2001–2006. Strategic paper from the National Arts Centre.

Securing the Future. Performing-arts discussion paper for the Australian government, Canberra, July 1999.

Snyder, Joel. *Crossing Boundaries: Where Artists and Art Forms Meet*. National Endowment for the Arts, Washington, DC, 1990.

Stern, Mark J., and Susan C. Seifert. *Community Revitalization and the Arts in Philadelphia*. Working Paper #8, University of Pennsylvania School of Social Work, Social Impact of the Arts Project, 1994.

Tusa, John. "Thou Shalt Worship the Arts for What They Are." Speech delivered at the Guthrie Theatre, Minneapolis. Edited version reprinted in *Spiked*, August 29, 2002.

"UNESCO Universal Declaration on Cultural Diversity." Paris: UNESCO, November 2001.

Upitis, Rena, and Katharine Smithrim. *Learning Through the Arts: National Assessment, 1999–2002, Final Report*. Royal Conservatory of Music, Toronto, 2003.

Van der Ploeg, F. *Culture as Confrontation: Principles and Cultural Policy in 2001–2004*. Policy discussion paper by the Dutch State Secretary for Education, Science and Culture, October 2000.

Venturelli, Shalini. *From the Information Economy to the Creative Economy: Moving Culture to the Center of International Public Policy*. Center for Arts and Culture, Washington, DC, 2001.

WMF Consulting Associates. *The Impact of Canada Council Individual Artist Grants on Artist Careers*. Study for the Canada Council for the Arts, March 2000.

Wong, Milton. *Made in Canada: The Origins and Potential of Multiculturalism for Educators*. Simon Fraser University, November 2, 2001.

Articles (selected)

Bemis, Alec Hanley. "Playtime." *LA Weekly*, March 29, 2002.

Berkeley, Michael. "Not Fade Away." *Guardian*, October 26, 2002.

Boyle, James. "Acting the Part." *The Scotsman*, December 17, 2002.

———. "Young at Art." *The Scotsman*, December 19, 2002.

Brustein, Robert. "The Four Horsemen of the Anti-Culture." *Partisan Review* 69, no. 4 (2002).

Caldwell, Rebecca. "Is Kids' Theatre on the Right Track?" *Globe and Mail,* December 12, 2002.

Clemens, Jason, and Niels Veldhuis. "Canada's Fatal Conceit." *Ottawa Citizen,* September 9, 2003.

Colbert, François. "Entrepreneurship and Leadership in Marketing the Arts." *International Journal of Arts Management* 6, no. 1 (fall 2003).

Cowie, William. "Fragmentation and the New Risk Discourse: Implications for Governance." *Optimum Online* (the journal of public sector management), December 2002.

Davidson, Justin. "Everything Old Is New Again." *Andante,* May 14, 2002.

Desbarats, Peter. "Who Needs Cultural Armour?" *Globe and Mail,* June 12, 2003.

Farrell, Christopher. "Art for Art's Sake? No, the Economy's." *BusinessWeek Online,* August 7, 2003. http://www.businessweek.com/.

Fischer, Hervé. "En attendant le huitième art, le rêve de l'oevre totale." *Le Devoir,* November 18, 2002.

Garreau, Joel. "The Call of Beauty, Coming In Loud and Clear." *Washington Post,* February 19, 2002.

Graham, Bill. "Culture Is the Face of Canada Abroad." *Hill Times,* October 7, 2002.

Hamblen, Karen A. "Theories and Research That Support Art Instruction for Instrumental Outcomes." *Theory into Practice* 32, no. 4, Ohio State University (1993).

Higgins, Charlotte. "All-rapping, All-kicking Dreams." *Guardian,* June 29, 2003.

Hobday, John. "Reality Check: Time for a Period of 'Creative Consolidation.'" *International Journal of Arts Management* 5, no. 1 (Fall 2002).

Iyer, Pico. "The Last Refuge: On the Promise of New Canadian Fiction." *Harper's,* June 2002.

Kaiser, Michael M. "How to Save the Performing Arts." *Washington Post,* December 29, 2002.

Kennedy, Maev. "Free Museums a Resounding Success." *Guardian,* January 1, 2003.

Kettle, Martin. "Let's Make an Opera." *Guardian,* November 22, 2002.

Kolb, Bonita M. "The Effect of Generational Change on Classical Music Concert Attendance and Orchestras' Responses in the UK and US." *Cultural Trends* 41, Policy Studies Institute, London (August 2002).

Kriedler, John. "Leverage Lost: The Nonprofit Arts in the Post-Ford Era." *In Motion* magazine, April 2003.

Lacey, Liam. "This Is a New Country." *Globe and Mail,* September 5, 2002.

McIntyre, Scott. "Literary Life Support." *Maclean's,* June 3, 2002.

Magnet, Myron. "What Use Is Literature?" *City Journal,* Manhattan Institute, Summer 2003.

Mathur, Ashok. "Race Poetry: An Eh-ditorial." *Prairie Fire* 21, no. 4 (March 2001).

Mihlar, Fazil. "Cultural Community Needs Tough Love." *National Post,* June 20, 2003.

Milner, Jenifer. "Arts Impact." Series of articles for the newsletter of Vancouver's Alliance for Arts and Culture, July 1998–December 1999.

———. "Arts Impact: Helping Us Determine Who We Are." *Performing Arts in Canada* 33, no. 4 (Summer 2002).

Milroy, Sarah. "Human Nature's Lab Tech." *Globe and Mail,* November 14, 2002.

Neuman, Johanna. "A Novel Idea Takes Wing in the Windy City." *Los Angeles Times,* February 17, 2002.

Petrunic, Josipa. "Renaissance Now." *Globe and Mail,* August 7, 2001.

Porter, Roy. "Culture and the City." *Daily Telegraph,* January 22, 2001.

Postrel, Virginia. "The Aesthetic Imperative." *Wired,* issue 11.07, July 2003.

Putnam, Robert D. "Bowling Together." *The American Prospect,* February 11, 2002.

Rabinovitch, Victor. "Method and Success in Canada's Cultural Policies." *Queen's Quarterly* 106, no. 2 (Summer 1999).

Richer, Shawna. "A New Face among Art Prizes." *Globe and Mail,* December 9, 2002.

Root-Bernstein, R. "For the Sake of Science, the Arts Deserve Support." *The Chronicle of Higher Education* 43 (1997).

Rusbridger, Alan. "Who's to Blame for Britney?" *Guardian,* May 8, 2003.

Saint-Pierre, Guy. "Business Must Come to the Aid of Public Schools." *Globe and Mail,* May 8, 2000.

Smith, Richard. "Spend (Slightly) Less on Health and More on the Arts." *British Medical Journal* (December 2002).

Todd, Douglas. "God in the Marketplace." Five-part series, *Vancouver Sun,* July–August 2003.

Various authors. "Paying the Piper: Arts Philanthropy in Canada." Six-part series, *Globe and Mail,* December 7–13, 2002.

Watson, Karen Joan. "The Art of Revitalizing Communities." *Forum,* May/June 2000.

Wilson-Smith, Anthony. "The Irony of Our Identity Crisis." *Maclean's,* May 20, 2002.

Winterson, Jeanette. "The Secret Life of Us." *Guardian,* November 25, 2002.

Wolpert, Lewis. "Which Side Are You On?" *Observer* (London), March 10, 2002.

BARRY PETERSON

MAX WYMAN is a Vancouver-based writer, critic and commentator. He has written a number of books on Canadian culture, among them *Dance Canada: An Illustrated History* and *Evelyn Hart: An Intimate Biography*. He has been dance, music and drama critic for the *Vancouver Sun* and the *Province* and was founding editor of the *Sun's* "Review of Books." His arts commentaries have been heard on CBC Radio since 1975, and he has contributed extensively to publications ranging from *The New York Times* to *The Canadian Encyclopedia*.

Max Wyman has taught critical writing and dance history at universities in Canada and across Europe. A former member of the board of the Canada Council for the Arts, he is currently president of the Canadian Commission for UNESCO. In 2001, he was named an Officer of the Order of Canada, and in 2003 he received an Honorary D. Litt. from Simon Fraser University.